Alexander Balloch Grosart, William Loe

The Songs of Sion of Dr. William Loe, (1620)

Alexander Balloch Grosart, William Loe

The Songs of Sion of Dr. William Loe, (1620)

ISBN/EAN: 9783337007867

Printed in Europe, USA, Canada, Australia, Japan

Cover: Foto ©Lupo / pixelio.de

More available books at **www.hansebooks.com**

MISCELLANIES

OF

The Fuller Worthies' Library.

THE
SONGS OF SION

OF

DR. WILLIAM LOE,

(1620);

Edited, with Memorial-Introduction and Notes,

BY THE

REV. ALEXANDER B. GROSART,

ST. GEORGE'S, BLACKBURN, LANCASHIRE.

PRINTED FOR PRIVATE CIRCULATION.
1870.

Memorial-Introduction.

ELL-NIGH every-body I should suppose, has heard in one way or another, the pulpit-story of two clergymen preaching in the same church on the same day and as candidates for the same post, their names being respectively '*Adam*' or Adams and '*Loe*'. The latter as the story runs, preached in the morning and took for text—with a tacit gibe at his announced successor, '*Adam!* where art thou?'. The former, not to be outdone, responded in the afternoon, with kindred name-play, '*Lo!* here am I'. Who the 'Adam' was, (or Adams: for it is sometimes the one spelling and sometimes the other) tradition hath forgotten. It might have been (if chronology agreed) quaint and audacious-witted THOMAS ADAMS of the immortal 'Sermons': (not the later Adam of the "Private Thoughts".) LYSONS says the 'Loe' was our present Worthy, giving as his authority a tractate yclept "Perfect Passages" dated 16th April, 1645—diligently but fruitlessly sought for by me.[1] THOMAS FULLER or EDWARD BOTELER or WILLIAM WORSHIP, never would have hesitated to make the jest, meaning no harm: and the impression made on myself by the books and single 'Sermons' of our Loe, is that he was of much the same make of intellect and temperament with these, and perhaps a dash of SOUTH. So that we may accept the long-told, variously-fathered anecdote, as really belonging to him in his younger days. From some ultra-serious folks the story may fetch a groan, even the anathema of 'profane': but it was'nt so, only o' the age irrepressibility of a nimble wit. Then what saith Sir Toby? "Dost thou think, because thou art virtuous, there shall be no more cakes and ale"? (Twelfth Night, ii. 3) or to paraphrase it, 'Because thou knowest not the bewitchment and inevitableness of a pun, is thy genial brother to be mis-judged?'. Enter right welcome, then, Dr. William Loe, with a smile i' thy face and mirth on thy lips. None the less a true and good and '*serious*' man that thou didst 'dearly love thy jest'.

The name is spelled by himself 'Loe' and 'Leo': for there is no doubt that ANTHONY-A-WOOD is correct, in regarding the two as one, in

---

[1] Lyson's Environs of London (1st edn.) Vol. I. p 293.

the places of their occurring. Twice at least it is given as 'Leo' viz: (*a*) in the Funeral-sermon —a remarkable one on a remarkable man—of Dr. Daniel Featley (1645) and the further designation "sometimes (= sometime) Preacher at Wandsworth in Surrey" (*b*) in his signature while Prebendary of Gloucester to certain "chapter-acts". From other sources we know—as will appear in the sequel—our Loe to have been "Preacher at Wandsworth" and "Prebendary at Gloucester". Hence the identification is certain. His friend Featley had the *alias* of 'Fairclough' in like manner.¹

I have not been able to trace either birth-place or birth-date of our "sweet Singer" and Divine. Probably he was of Kent: for in his Featley 'sermon', incidentally naming a 'knight' (Sir George Sands) of the county, he speaks of him as 'my countryman of Kent' (p. 24). The Fasti Oxonienses (edn. by Bliss I. 275, 285, 335, 381, 382) supplies the *data* of his University career at Oxford:

---

¹ The funeral-sermon is full of anecdote of rare value to a biographer of Featley: and besides, Loe has various allusions to his own travels and experiences: and lovingly names his own son William as of Trinity College, Cambridge. See page 23 of this Sermon.

Among B. A's, 5th Novr. 1597: " Will. Loe of St. Alb. Hall.

Among M. A's, 14th June 1600: *ibid. ibid.*

Among B. D's, 22, Feby. 1609-1610 " Will. Loe of St. Alb. Hall did supplicate for the same degree, but whether he was admitted, appears not ".

Among B. D's, 8th June 1618: ' Will. Loe of Mert. Coll. sometimes of St. Alban's Hall.

Among D. D's 8th June 1618: ' Will. Loe of Mert. Coll. a compounder and an accumulator.'

When he took his degree of M. A., ANTHONY-A-WOOD in his *Athenæ Oxonienses* (edition by Bliss, III., 183-4) states that " he was much in esteem for Latin, Greek, and human learning." This was (as *supra*) in 1600. In the same year he must have been Vicar of Churcham, Gloucester: for in its Parish-Register as still preserved, I find from the present Vicar (Rev. George C. Hall, M. A.,) record is made that Dr. Loe transcribed the entries "ex veteri libro cartaceo" in the 42nd year of Elizabeth, *id est*, 1600. Under 1593 there is in his handwriting a note " Finis veteris libri cartacei " : but the ' Fasti' degree-dates seem to shew that he could not have been so early in orders as 1594. Therefore the meaning must be that an ancient Register was transcribed by him that ended in 1593, while the genuine one commenced from 1594. "Soon after", (1600) he was made Master of the College School in Gloucester: and was instituted "on the 30th September, 1602" Prebendary of Gloucester [Cathedral 5th Stall]. He was sub-dean in 1605. Probably these offices were held simultaneously as not very onerous pluralities.[1] The Churcham Register further informs us, that he was married while in possession of that 'living', as under 1612 we read: "Sept, 27th, Hester the daughter of William Loe, Vicar, was baptised."[2] The absence of signatures to the successive annual entries prevents our determining the period of his incumbency. Not until 1633 does a signature appear, that of Francis Hathway—another form of the maiden name of MRS. WILLIAM SHAKESPEARE—by which date Loe was most certainly elsewhere.[3] The 'College School' of Gloucester has been very neglectful of its history, as have also been

---

[1] Consult Fosbrooke, and also Rudder's History of Gloucester, (p. 169).

[2] Rev. Samuel Lysons, F. S. A., of Hampstead Court, in a letter to me, from Archdeacon Furney's MSS. in his possession.

[3] I have very cordially to thank the Rev. George C.

the county Historians. There is a tantalizing absence of dates: indeed the Records do not go beyond the Restoration of Charles II. WOOD mentions that JOHN LANGLEY succeeded our 'Master' but not the years of either, while Fosbrooke gives two Masters between Loe and Langley, viz., THOMAS POTTER (1605) and John Clark (1612).[1] It needed a man of brain to be 'Master' of such a School as that of Gloucester: and it were interesting to know the more famous 'boys' of it. When will our county-Historians understand, that these are the kind of facts that are of substantive and abiding value,—not mere 'endless genealogies' of noble-ignoble nonentities,—pyramid-wise, all

---

Hall, M. A., of Churcham, for his great kindness in answering my enquiries.

[1] I must, as in last note, equally thank Dr Washbourne of Gloucester and Rev. Samuel Lysons, as above, for their like interest and attention. The latter writes me "Fosbrooke does not give the date of Loe's appointment to the Cathedral School, but places him between Elias Wrench who was appointed in 1588, and Thomas Potter who was appointed in 1605." Perhaps when appointed sub-dean in 1605 Loe resigned his Mastership. See above and onward where in the "Merchant Reall" he says under date 1619-20, that he had been "one of the masters seventeene yeares". This goes back to 1602-3.

too often, broad-based and a 'mere point' at last.

Probably the central thing of our Worthy's life took place in 1618, in which year the Cathedral-Records tell us, he obtained a "testimonial from the Chapter to become Pastor of the English Church [at Hamburgh" or as it was spelled 'Hamborough'. This at once links him to the subject-matter of our reprint, the "Songs of Sion"—the manifold dedications of which keep before us the fact that he was the 'Minister' of the 'Merchant-adventurers' of the once and still renowned city. From the Introduction to an exceedingly rare if not uniquely-preserved copy of a book of his, the 'Merchant reall", now in the Public Library of Hamburg, we learn that he let a year and a half pass before he decided to accept the post. These are his words: "I demurred after mine election, a whole yeare and a halfe, and begged of God to resolve me touching my coming unto you". He seems to have been unwilling to leave England: for he continues as follows: "and now being come, I doe protest in the sight of God and His holy angells, that I come not unto you with any Italianated hart of implaceability that cannot be appeased, nor with any Hispanialized hart of Iesuited novelty, nor with a Frenchified hart of singulaiitie, nor yet

with a Dutchified hart of neutrality (all which
I speake not as of any nationall disgrace, for the
finest cambrick may have many fretts and frayes)
but I am come with a good and an honest Englishe
hart of orthodox and catholike sincerity." At this
time (1620)[1] the same introduction informs us, he
had been "22 years a member of the English
church, and 17 years a teacher in the school".
This is in harmony with the Parish register of
Churcham by which we dated his appointment
there, 1600 or thereby.[2]

The Merchant-adventurers of England to whom
Loe acted as chaplain, were an important company.
Previously to 1618 they moved about a good deal,
according as the 'markets' for their imports and
exports led them. Thus they are found at Embden,
Middleburgh, Stade, and elsewhere. The second
place 'Middleborough' will remind the bookish
reader of a number of quaint old title-pages
bearing quaint old Puritan names, and of certain
bibliographical rarities that freely fetch weight
for weight in gold, as SIR JOHN DAVIES' Epigrams
in association with MARLOWE's Ovid's 'Elegies'.
It will also recall silver-tongued Joshua Sylvester

---

[1] Dr. Klose seems to misdate from 1618.
[2] See Note at end of this Memorial-Introduction.

—agent of the 'Merchant-adventurers' there—
who by the way inscribes his " Tobacco Battered "
to our Loe, in the following Sonnet:

> " To my reverend and worthy friend, Mr. William Loe,
> Batchelor of Divinity.
>
> Lo, what you love and this chimera's hate,
>   Care of my friends, compassion of my kin ;
>   Zeal of God's glory, horror of this sin ;
>   My soveraign's service, honour of our State :
> Lo, what all these had pow'r to propagate !
>   (Perhaps more hardly then my hope had bin,
>   When first this theam YOU GAVE ME TO BEGIN)
>   Besides my way, beyond my waining date.
> Lo, therefore, whether well or ill I fare ;
>   Whether the doubtfull field I win or lose ;
>   In fame, or shame, YOU needs must have a share,
> Who on my weakness did this weight impose.
>   Like Moses therefore lift your hands on hie,
>   That *Joshuah's* hand may have the victory."
>   (Works, 1611, p. 572).

In 1618 the Hamburg authorities arranged for the Association settling permanently in their city. A contract was entered into and 'incorporation, given. LINGARD, of all our English historians, slightly notices these 'Merchant-adventurers'. It were surely worth-while for some Englishman to get at the facts of these pioneers of England's now world-embracing commerce.

One of the title-pages bears the date '1620': so that he was not long in 'imping his wing' for a poetic flight. The Epistles-Dedicatory bear witness to the warm, mutual respect of the 'Merchant-adventurers' and their Chaplain. There were evidently among them 'gentle' men, in the real and not merely titular sense. These Epistles also reveal a fine fervour of concern for the spiritual welfare of his 'dear Masters' and 'table-fellows'.

How long he remained in Hamburg, I have failed to ascertain: but the probability is,—though the many dedications of the "Songs of Sion" give no hint of intended departure,—that he did not remain very many years subsequent to 1620.

From Lyson's Environs of London¹, under 'Putney', there is a note of 'William Leo as 'curate' and Preacher in 1624; in which year his signature occurs as "Preacher at Putney". This Leo is identified as Wood and ourselves do, with Loe. Perhaps his Hamburg residence made him uncertain in his orthography, seeing that Löwe in German means a Lion *i. e.* Leo and Loe are just an abbrevi-

---

¹ Vol. I. p 416: same authority and reference for our opening anecdote.

ation of Lowe. One of the sermon-books already
quoted from, is dedicated "to the right Worshipfull Sr Thomas *Lowe*, Knight, Governour," as
well as to "the Deputies, assistants and Generall-
tie, of that anncient, much famous, and most
worthy companie of Merchants Adventurers, residing at London, Hamborough, Middleborough,
&c. &c. There is no claim of relationship made.
Let name-enquirers follow up the clue presented.[1]
Besides Putney, as we saw, the Funeral-sermon
for Featley, bears that the Preacher was 'sometime'
of "Wandsworth in Surrey". I have had most
willing helpers there, in the excellent present
Incumbent and other friends[2]: but the result of
long-continued researches is provokingly meagre.
Nevertheless the dates are of importance, albeit
they merely authenticate the Incumbency and
shew descendants afterwards. At the foot of the
page ending 5th March 1636, under Marriages, in
Parish Register, there are certain signatures viz :
" Wm. Leo, Tho. Ballard, Willi. Ashenden", the

---

[1] In the Wandsworth Registers, there is a baptism of
a Thomas *Lowe's* daughter Rebecca : 13th. June 1645.

[2] I must name Dr. J. T. Harris of Englefield Green,
Staines, and the Parish-Clerk of Wandsworth, Mr. Willson,
—the latter an intelligent and antiquarianly disposed
custodier of the Registers.

first no doubt the Vicar, the other Churchwardens. The same signatures re-appear in the register of Baptisms of July, 1636, to November, 1638, with the substitution of Blagrave for Ballard on two occasions. The same also in the Burials from April 1636 to October, 1638. Further: as in the Register of Burials there is an entry of the interment of "Mr. Robert Allen, vicar of Wandsworth" on 16th June 1631, our Loe probably succeeded him. Under baptisms 16th September 1646 is entered, "Isaack, the sonne of Isaack Loe". Another Vicar, "Mr. Hugh Roberts" had a son John baptized 2d Novr. 1645. Probably he succeeded Loe: and probably Loe held the 'living' until his death in 1645, though he seems to have been resident in the City (of London). As "Preacher" at Putney and as having been appointed "Chaplain to the King"—poor reward of a long-tried loyalty in 'evil days' (to him)—he would require to 'abide' in the Metropolis. There at last, in all likelihood in a ripe old age, he died and was buried, in no less sacred a sleeping-place than Westminster. Wood was ignorant of his death-date: John Walker in his famous (or infamous) "Sufferings of the Clergy" names 1648, and so Fosbrooke and others. But inasmuch as Roberts was Vicar at Wandsworth at close of

1645, I had assigned that year for his death independent of an interesting discovery of my friend Colonel Chester—one of many tid-bits that have turned up in the course of his unexampled persistency of research among our national Registers I will allow him to put the matter before the Reader as he has done in a letter to myself, as follows : " One of the most perplexing entries I found in the Westminster Abbey Registers was this burial " 1645 . Sept. 21. Dr. Lee.—in the South side of the Church, near the Vestry door." I could find nothing of this Dr. Lee. There was no monument and no inscription recorded in any of the printed books. All the Doctors *Lee*, whether of Law, Medicine or Theology or even Music that I could trace, died either before or after that date. And I could find no Will of a Dr. Lee. The man haunted me from December 1866 down to last Spring, when after a great deal of trouble, I got hold of the Wills and Administrations of the Dean and Chapter of Westminster, which had been hid away for a century in a lawyer's office in Doctors Commons, and at last was claimed by and taken to the principal Registry of Probate. Among these, to my great joy, I found that on the 13th of November, 1645, letters of Administration were granted by the

Dean and Chapter on the Estate of " William Loe, *alias* Loe, S.T.P. " late of the city of Westminster, to Elizabeth Basset, a creditor." The information was meagre enough: but here was clearly my troublesome 'Dr. Loe'". I do not think there can be any doubt as to the identity; and the explanation of the later date given by Walker of the " Sufferings"—a book that swarms with blunders intentional and inadvertent—Le Neve in his " Fasti ", and similar authorities, is, that they inferred the death-date from the accession of the new incumbent to his stall: whereas the ' troubles ' of the period kept it vacant for some years.

We have found that at Churcham Loe had a daughter baptized ' HESTER '. We know not his wife's name or family. He had at least one other child, a son, who bore his own name and who appears to have passed a brilliant University career, being of renowned ' Trinity College, Cambridge ', not of Oxford like his father. In the Funeral-sermon on Featley preached under the shadow of his own near-coming death, Dr. Loe makes loving mention of this son William: and the paternal regard must have been reciprocated filially: for in an exquisite specimen of penmanship (were it no more it should be a literary gem) I happen to possess, viz, a small MS. volume, antiquely bound, consisting of 'readings' in Plautus and other of the classics, together with at least one somewhat striking original (Latin) poem that I shall include as a parrallel in my edition of RICHARD CRASHAW, there is prefixed a very long and glowing Epistle-dedicatory, to his father. In this the language labours in setting forth his worth and genius and among many other things, his 'poetic' fame. It is scarcely worth-while translating this (Latin) Epistle: but as Loe jr. was a son of 'Trinity' I intend placing the M.S. under the custody of my friend Mr. W. Aldis Wright, Librarian of Trinity College, that it may be accessible to inquirers. The son not the father, was author of the sets of Latin verses contained in the "Carmen Natalitium ad cunas illustrissimæ Principis Elizabethæ decantatum intra Navitatis Dom. solennia per humiles Cantabrigiæ Musas" (1635).[1]

---

[1] Colonel Chester sends me the following extract from the Parish Registers of St. Martins in the Fields: Marriage 5 June 1642: William Loe and Margaret Shipton, both of Westminster". Probably Loe *filius*. Further he writes "in the cloisters of Westminster Abbey was buried 1 Mch. 1676-7, according to the Register " Colonel Hercules Lowe" who in an unofficial Register kept by one of the Minor Canons, usually more correct than the early

As a contribution to Bibliography I have now to furnish a full and probably complete list of the Writings of our Worthy in chronological order.

1. The Ioy of Ierusalem and Woe of Worldings. A Sermon preached at Paul's Crosse the 18 of Iune 1609. By William Loe, Batchelour of Diuinity, and Prebendarie of the Cathedral Church of Glocester. London, printed by T. Haueland for C. Knight and I. Harrison, and are to be sold in Pauls Churchyard at the signe of the holy Lambe. 1609. [sq. 18mo.] Collation: Title-page, Epistle-dedicatory 2 leaves—Sermon 63 leaves. [Text St. John, xvii. 9.]

2. Come and See, The Blisse of Brightest Beavtie, Shining ovt of Sion in Perfect Glorie. Being the Summe of foure Sermons preached in the Cathedrall Church of Glocester at commandment of Superiours. By William Loe. Imprinted at London by Richard Field and Matthew Law. 1614 [4to.] **** The Epistle-dedicatory is dated "The Colledge of Glow. Febru. 20. 1611". Wood misreads "The Bible the brighest beauty &c. and whereas it is 'William Loe' simply, by

---

official Register, is given as "Hercules Loe". It is possible that this may have been of our Loe's line: but nothing seems known of him.

adding " D in divinity, sometime preacher at Wandsworth in Surrey" the foot-note from Wanley, throws the whole chronology of the Life into confusion, as I found on searching at Wandsworth from 1614 onward, instead of the later date of the incumbency. I had not seen " Come and See " at the time, and it is plain Wood had not, and also that Wanley confounded it with the funeral-sermon for Featley.

3. The Mysterie of Mankind, Made into a Manual, or the Protestants Portuize [= Breviary] reduced into Explication, Application, Invocation, tending to Illumination, Sanctification, Devotion, being the sum of seven Sermons. Preached at S. Michaels in Cornehill, London, by William Loe, Doctor of Divinity, Chaplain to his sacred Majesty, and Pastor Elect, and allowed by authority of Superiours, of the English Church at Hamborough in Saxonie. 1 Cor 3. 23. All are yours and yee Christ's, and Christ God's. London, Printed by Bernard Alsop for George Fayerheard, and are to be sold at his shoppe at the South side of the Exchange. 1619 [12mo] Collation: Title-page—299 numbered pages, 49 unnumbered, a blank page, a page of errata, and five blank leaves.

4. The Merchant reall, Preached by William

iam Loe, Doctour of Divinitie, Chaplain of the King's sacred majestic, and Pastour of the English church of Merchants-Adventurers residing at Hamborough in Saxonie. Matth. 16, 26. What is a man profited if he shall purchase the whole world and lose his owne soule? or what shall a man give in exchange for his soule? Printed at Hamborough by Paule Lang, Ann. Domini, 1620. [4to] Collation: Title-page— 6 unnumbered and 106 numbered pages.

5. The Songs of Sion: See our present reprint, for general title-page and separate titles.

6. Vox Clamantis: a still voice to the three thrice honourable estates of Parliament: and in them to all the soules of this our Nation, of what state or condition soever they be. By William Loe, Doctor of Divinitie, and chaplaine to the king's most excellent Majestic. Printed by T. S. for John Teage, and are to be sold at the signe of the Golden Ball in Paul's Churchyard. [4to.]

7. A Sermon on Psalm xlv., 3., preached at Whitehall, with a dedication to the King. 1622. [4to.] *∗* I find a note of this in my *memoranda*, but have mislaid the full title-page.

8. The King's Shoe Made and Ordained to trample and to treade downe Edomites: to teach in briefe, what is Edom's doome; what the care-

full condition of a King; what the loyall submission of a subiect, and what proiects are onely to best purpose. Deliuered in a Sermon before the King at Theobalds, October the ninth, 1622. By William Loe, Doctour of Diuinity, Chaplaine to his sacred majesty in ordinary. London, 1623. [4to]. Collation: Title-page— Epistle-dedicatory 3 leaves and pp. 45. [Text Psalm lx, 8].

9. A Sermon preached at Lambeth, Apr. 21, 1645 at the Funerall of that learned and polemical Divine, Dan. Featley, Doctor in Divinity, late preacher there: with a short relation of his Life and Death, by William Leo, Doctor in Divinity, sometime Preacher at Wandesworth in Surrey. Lond. Printed for Richard Royston, dwelling in Ivie-lane, 1645. [4to]
⁎ Prefixed is a singular copper-plate engraving of Dr. Featley in his shroud, his noble face bare. 2 pp latin verse and pp 32.

The first of this List " The Ioy of Ierusalem " has escaped all our bibliograpical authorities, including even the omniverous Anthony a-Wood. As the text prepares us to expect, it is an exposition of the crown of all Prayers, recorded in the 17th chapter of St. John: and a somewhat startling request is made as to the time intended to be occupied. Speaking of The Lord's praying, the Preacher says " whereunto I earnestly desire you to attend as to one of the Songs of Sion and the joy of Ierusalem : and therein I shall pray you to watch and wait the first houre, to the joy of your hearts, who truely seeke and serue the Lord. As for the second houre, the woe of the worldlings—His not praying ['I pray not for them '] shall be denounced, that all flesh may tremble and all people perceive the glorious salvation of our God." 'Two hours' preaching at a stretch! Yet judging from the little book nobly were they occupied. Our modern audiences have too queasy stomachs to digest such 'strong meat'. I cull two small morsels from this sermon worthy of its renowned pulpit— " What was *propositum* in God the Father is *depositum* in Jesus Christ the Son and *repositum* in expectation of the faithfull" (2 Timothy iv. 8.). Then worked out from a Father, this thought seems to me to lift off the ultra-Calvinistic horror thrown over the words 'I pray not for the world '— 'Here He prays for His friends not naming His enemies : at the Cross He prayed for His enemies not naming His friends.' There surely we have a golden ray shot direct from the Sun of Righteousness. The 4to ' The Merchant reall ' Anthony a-Wood states he had never seen, and I do not know of a single copy in any public or private Library of our own Country. I have been fortunate enough to trace it to the Public Library of Hamburg; where it is regarded as one of the rarities of a Library holding many treasures. The ' Merchant Reall ' forms the text of an exceedingly interesting Paper on Loe by Dr. C. R. W. Klose, Secretary to the Public Library, Hamburg, which appeared in "No. 11: July 31st, of the Serapeum" a literary journal published and still publishing at Leipzig. Dr. Klose adds nothing, unfortunately, to the biography of our Worthy, though surely research in the *archives* of the city should have yielded new materials elucidative and illustrative of the "Merchant-adventurers"—but I have to thank him for leading me to a knowledge of (apparently) the one surviving exemplar of a valuable book. To the prompt courtesy of a successor of Dr. Loe—the present British Chaplain of Hamburg, the Rev. C. F. Weidemann, M.A.—I am indebted for copious extracts from the " Merchant Reall" and from No 3, the " Mysterie of Maukind "—the Bodleian copy of which is unique in England.

I have already given the 'greeting ' of the Epistle-dedicatory of the " Merchant-reall". The

Epistle itself explains the title and furnishes certain auto-biographic deails, as follow: "Right worshipfull and much endeered in the Lord. Promise is debt, and debt is due. The dutie of my service, and the debt of my promise, I nowe make bold to tender unto you all. The promise which I made unto you at London when I began this taske, by God's permission I haue finished at Hambrough. and now tender performance. It is not many yeares since that a learned Doctour who is nowe with God, preaching in Court at an honorable marriage, out of the Proverbs, 'She is like a merchant shippe that bringeth her merchandize from afarre'. (Prov. 31, 14.) called his sermon 'The marchant-royall': I haue termed this the 'Marchant Reall.' For that royaltie is is upheld by Realtie. And wise men wishe euer rather to be Realls than Nominalls". Further, as addressing Merchants he has this *bit* on their 'calling': "I knowe noe condition of men more happie then merchants. Their veary youth is accompanied with many and many fold experienced trialls, both by sea and land, which may make them prudent. Their mature age is blessed with a plentifull portion, which may make them thankfull, and their old age affordeth a very surplusage of marvellous fulness, which may satisfie them".

In the body of the work we come on these personal *data*, used earlier by us and as there noted slightly corrective of Dr. Klose : " Mine enterance unto you here, is and was, both civill and honest. First by free election of your own fellowshipe. Secondly by approbation of the State whence I came. Thirdly by recommendation of his sacred majestie, under his own hand, who pleased to grace me, his unworthy servant, with his royall letters, and of the most reverend archbishop of Canterbury, who patriarchally tended your peace. Fourthly with attestation from the famous Universitie of Oxford under their seale, and from the Cathedral Church, where I have been a member two and twenty yeares, and one of the masters, seventeene yeeres." (pp. 1-2). Take now a few quaint sentences gleaned here and there from the " Merchant Reall ". Of man's natural condition he says " When we come into the world, our frends cover our shame with raggs, and in the end when we goe out of the world, they doe the like. All of us are Mephibosheths, lame on both legs, both in our love to God and in our charity one to another. We are all Lazaruses full of sores, and lie begging at the gate of God's rich mercie" (p 22). These *characteristics* of various countries are noticeable : " The sea and the earth, those two grand caskets of God's treasures are in severall places diversely furnished. So that one country seemeth as it were the granary of the world. So Sicilie was called the granary of the Romane State. Another, the cellar of the world, as the Canarie Islands. Another the orchard of the world, as Lombardy in Ittaly so accompted. Another the arcenall of the world, as Russia and Norway are esteemed, espetially for cordage and materialls of shipping" (pp 23, 24). Here are oddly put antitheses, having the Fullerian flavour: "All pretious stones procede from one and the selfe same matter, which is the earth, and yet see what great difference there is betweene the vile and the pretious, between the currant and the counterfaite: even so among the sonnes of men, all are made of the one and the same matter: yett what difference there is betwixt man and man of the same mould, betweene brother and brother of the same bloud, even as much as betweene Simon Magus and Simon Peter, Cephas and Caiphas, Judas the traytor and Jude the apostle, yea what difference is in one man when God takes him into his hand, as of a persecuting Saule to make him a preaching Paule" (p. 37). So too this: "We teach onlie that good workes have no justifying quality in themselves before God, but that faith only is like

John the divine leaning on Christ's breasts, and good works like St. Peter, that follow after Christ. Faith the bride goeth into the chamber, yea into the bed of her beloued, where the handmaids come not. Faith the bride, good works the handmaids. Faith the roote, good workes the fruite. Faith only necessary to justification, good workes to salvation" (p. 41). Perhaps the truth had been truer put if it had run 'We are saved by faith not by works, but are saved unto or in order to work for the Master'. This, reminds of Bacon: "Be directed therefore to recompence noe man evill for evill, as Joab did Abner, for that's a poore spirit; much lesse evill for good, as Judas did to Christ, for that's a divell's spirit. Nay, if you doe recompense good with good, as Ahasueresh did Mordicai, it is but common justice; but to overcome evill with goodnes is more than to preach, or to doe a miracle, or to cast out a divell" (p. 46). Here is a *pat* application: "Our case is as the case of Aaron which had a robe, bells, a tunacle, an ephod, the Urim and Thumim, and blew silke and fine linnen, yet all these were none of his owne, but ornaments ordayned by God, to be put upon him. So have we no pretiousnes in our selves". (p 74). So this: "Oh what a foolish thing is it to be carefull to keepe the chicken from the kite, the lamb from the wolfe, and the dove from the vermin, and to be carelesse to keepe our-selves from the devill." (p 91).

The "Mysterie of Mankinde" yields kindred quotable things: but we must content ourselves with three in all. First is a small pun in the Preface: "Let us therefore never listen to 'This I say, this thou sayest': but let us heare when the Lord sayeth, and let that αυτος εφα bee our religious ephod to put upon us." Next of the religious hypocrite: "Such are they that have Jacob's voice in prating of godlinesse, but Esau's hands in preaching unhappinesse. Such are they that professe a linzie woolsey religion, being hatefull to God because they are not reall, hatefull to the world because they are religious, albeit they be but in shew, and hurtfull to themselves, because they are hypocrites and decyve themselves with seeming godlinesse" (p 34). Then this of goodness: "Beleevers see even by the very glimpse of right reason, that nothing but man maketh account of greatnes. God doth not, for with him is no respect of persons; Nature doth not, for the children of princes are borne naked as well as the cottager's, and death assayleth the Court as well as the cart. Godlines only is that wherein God delighteth, and good men tender it as their breath: Godlinesse being the gracious mother and goodnesse the holy daughter." (p 38). Finally, the Preacher gives no very favourable 'report' of Church-audiences : "The more verecundious and modest wee are in this our hearing of God, and in our comming unto Him, the more bright and beautiful we are in His sacred sight . . . . But the manner is now with many to come as Sathan did—for company or custom or worse—[who] came also when the sons of God were assembled before him—to the divell's chappell, according to our English proverbe " Where God hath His Church, the divell hath his chappel." For even in the great assemblies, while some are there hearing the Word attentively, others sleep profoundly, while some reade, others prate, while some lift up their eyes to heaven, others point out the finger to note some vanity in the next pue, while some pray, others scoffe, while some sing others curse, while some sigh for their sinnes, others laugh at sinne, and while others sit harkening to the sermon unto the ende, others make hast to bee gone, and thinke every houre two, untill they hear the 'Peace of God' which they will scarce vouchsafe to take with them, nor the 'Grace of God' neither." (pp 231—2).

It were no hard matter to bring together from these and the other Sermons things worth remembrance. Enough however has been adduced to shew the 'manner of man' our Worthy was. I have intentionally refrained from quoting his vehement and ever-recurring flings at Popery, and equally have passed his fervid and softly-worded, tender prayers. The one reveals the strength of his hatred, the other his charity: and as prayer is a more potential and deep-reaching thing than sermon-making, one may rejoice that his 'Invocations' out-weigh his 'Imprecations'.

Of the "Songs of Sion" now reprinted, it needeth not that I say much. There are sweet, simple, pathetic strokes in these monosyllabled 'Songs' and a quiet, child-like directness that is to me very loveable. I have found them to grow on me, as your child's small words of question and wistful looks, grow and deepen before you. That is, the short, homely, common words, as you dwell on them, dilitate and speak grand things in a modest, most unconscious way. The fact that from beginning to end of the Verse, words of a single syllable alone are used, gives an unique character to the book: and altogether it is a humbly noticeable contribution to the History of the development of our poetic Literature. Our modern travestiers of the 'Pilgrim's Progress' and 'Robinson Crusoe' and other classics, adapted (so-called) for children, might improve their sorry work by turning to Loe's mono-syllables. As a book the 'Songs of Sion' is of extreme rarity. I know only of two exemplars, viz., in the British Museum and in the Bodleian. It is not at Hamburg.

ALEXANDER B. GROSART.

St. George's Blackburn,
    Lancashire.

NOTE.

I embrace the opportunity of this little space, to quote another dated statement from the opening of the Sermon for Featley: "It is not my mind nor meaning, neither was it ever my manner, I having now preached the Gospel seven and forty years, in Court, City, Country and beyond the Seas, to trouble mine auditories with any long or large beginnings" (p 1). 47 years from 1645, carries back to 1598. Cf. our Memorial-Introduction on Churcham. (pp 2—3).

From the encrease of materials while the "Songs of Sion" were being printed, the 22 pages left have proved insufficient: accordingly, I partly page only on one side, in order to keep the pagination continuous. G.

The Poems of Dr. Loe.

Note.

There is a general title-page to Dr. Lee's little volume, which is found only in the British Museum copy, not being in the Bodleian or any other known: "Songs of Sion, Set for the ioy of gods deere ones, who sitt here by the brookes of this worlds Babel, & weepe when they thinke on Hierusalem which is on highe. By W. L." [N. D.] and Mr. Haz'itt in his Hand-Book s. n. furnishes another: but it is only a partial enumeration of the separate title-pages: it ... its entirely "An hymne or song of seauen strains or strings" &c., and otherwise is imperfect, as our reprint shews. At each division of the little volume, there is a separate title-page and a separate Epistle-dedicatory. These are given in their own places. Collation: title-page and 115 leaves, having throughout, a number of blank pages, as marked. G.

An hymne or song
Of seauen straines, or strings
set to the tone of seaven sobs, and
sighes of a seauen times seauen sad
soule for sinne, and is to be song in
the tune of
I lift mine hart to thee.
Psal. 25. or
Flie soule vnto thy rest.
Seauen times a daie will I praie
to thee o god, and will praie thee
o lord for thy great gifts, and good
graces, both to me,
and mine.
Psalm CXIX.
When the spright of mā doth sighe,
and sob to god, and is lift vp on highe,
the spright of god doth bowe it
selfe to man in ioy,
and peace.
CYPRIAN.

Epistle-Dedicatory.

To his much esteemed good frend, Mr. JOHN POWELL, one of the assistants of the worthy cōpanie of the Marchants Aduenturers, residing at Hamborough.[1]

Grace, peace, and mercie be multiplied in Christ Iesu.

WORTHY frend. When Iuliā the Apostate infested the Church of God,[2] sōtimes by barbarous cruelty and somtimes by deuilish policie, among his other wicked practises, that was not the least nor the last, when he interdited the Christians all vse of bookes, both priuatly and publikely, for their children to learne,

---

[1] See our Memorial-introduction for notice of this Company G

[2] Usually as in general title-page *supra*, printed with a small 'g': but I don't repeat this. As usual all the Divine proper names (but not the pronouns, as they are so very numerous) and impersonations are given capitals. G.

excepte Poetry. It pleased Almighty God in that distresse of his Church to stirre vp a learned man, one Apollinarius, a singular Metaphrast, to put into heroicall Greeke verse all the psalmes of Dauid: by which blessing the children of God had vse and comfort of that booke of the psalme[s] and the tyrant's decree tooke noe hold of thē, because nowe it was become deuine poesie; and poetry they might read. Which shewes vnto vs God's especiall and singular providence for his Church vpon all occasions. And nowe, albeit— God be blessed—there is noe cause to complaine, either of any such apostaticall power—for we haue an apostolicall king—nor of any such wicked pollicy,—for we haue had kings and queēs, nursing fathers and nursing mothers of our Church; yet in these halcyon daies of ours, I haue presumed to metaphrase some passages of Dauid['s] psalmes, as an essay to know whether we might expresse our harts to God in our holy soliloquies, in mōasillables in our owne mother tongue or no. It being a receaued opinion amōgst many of those who seeme rather to be inditious than caprichious, that heretofore our English tongue in the true idiome thereof, consisted altogether of monosillables, vntill it came to be blended and mingled with the commixture

of exotique languages. And I my selfe haue
seene all the Lord['s] prayer vsed in the tyme of
John Wickleefe to be expressed in words of one sill-
able. And because God's children did reckon seauen
tymes seauen yeares before they could enioy their
yeare of Iubile, I haue made allusion in this
little Essay to tune forth seauē tymes seauen sad
sobbs for sinne, that when we haue spent the
remaynder of our wretched dayes of our pilgrim-
age here, God may in his mercie, wipe away
all teares from our eyes, and bring vs to our
eternall Iubile, in his glorious kingdome. Which
God grant to you, to me, and to all Christian
people for his owne rich mercie['s][1] sake, and the
satisfactory meritts of Iesus Christ our Lord,
Amen.

Written from my studie within the English
house at Hamborough, Jan. 24.

  Yours because you are of Christ.

          WILL: LOE.

---

[1] In this Epistle I have added the apostrophe: but note
the transition-forms, 'passages of Dauid psalmes' and
'the Lord prayer' and 'rich mercie sake'. Hereafter I
will not make the correction required by present grammatical usage, the more especially as the thing is common
to Spenser and other contemporaries. The Teares of
the Muses says "whom Nature selfe had made (l, 205)

and so elsewhere. Throughout I silently remove mere misprints, as 'lift' in above title-page is 'life' where however I have left 'tone', which probably ought to be 'tune'. A foreign Press explains such errata. G.

THE FIRST STRAINE.

LORD heare my suite, my plainte,   1
    That my soule makes to thee:
  Lord in thy truth one looke of grace
Grant in thy loue to me.

Lord see the moane I make,   2
    Looke on me in thy grace:
Let not my sighes come back in vaine
    But shewe to me thy face,

Loe I was borne in sinne;   3
    My kind, my shape, my all,
My stocke, my flocke, my selfe from birth
    O Lord from thee did fall

And I poore soule am sett   4
    In greefe, in paine, in woe ;
My sinnes come on, my soule doth faint,
    O quitt me of my foe.

My sinnes, the haires doe passe   5
    That are set on my head ;
My hart doth feare, and faint, and faile
    And I am as one dead.

Thus goe I greeud, and goord,   6
   And frett in hart, and spright:
Thus am I faint with feare and death,
   My sinnes they doe me fright.

The deeds that I haue done   7
   Are sett in vewe of eie;
My faults, my thoughts, my sinne, my shame
   Thy lawes, thy lookes, doe spie.

I. Sighe.

O that my thoughts. words, workes, and waies, were made so straight and right, that I might keepe thy lawes O Lord, all the daies and nights of my whole life: so should I be clere and cleane from the guilt of sinne and shame.

THE SECOND STRAINE.

GOD if thou shouldst waighe   1
   My waies and take a vewe,
I could not scape thy rod; thy wrath,
   I should in woe it rue.

O iudge me not I pray,   2
   O sheeld me from my fall;

For in thy sight none iust doth liue
 No none I say at all.

Large is thy loue to me, 3
 For it with thee I treate :
O grant me it for Christ, his sake,
 Gainst sinnes so huge, so great.

O Christ what wight doth knowe 4
 His sinne and faults of life ?
O cleanse me from my sinnes at once
 Which are in me most rife.

And keepe me Lord I craue 5
 Least sinnes doe ore me sway :
So shall I then be free, and faine
 To keepe thy lawe for aie.

This Lord of thee I beg, 6
 To thee I hold vp hands ;
And hart and soule, both thirst, and gape,
 As doth the drought in lands.

As maids doe watch and waite, 7
 On queenes, some grace to haue ;
So doe I Lord both day and night
 For grace both beg and craue.

II. Sight.

O that there were such an hart in me to feare thee, and to keepe all thy lawes that it might goe well with me and mine for aye.

THE THIRD STRAINE.

LORD, turne thee to thy grace 1
    That once thou shewedst to me!
  O saue me not for my good acts :
    I seeke, I sue to Thee.

My soule why dost thou faint? 2
    And art with greefe soe prest?
My hart, my mind, why doe you thus
    Fret sore within my brest

Trust soule to God for aye, 3
    And thou the time shalt see,
When thou shalt thinke, and thanke him still
    For health, and peace to thee.

For why, his wrath doth last, 4
    A space, and then doth slacke :
But in his face, and grace for aye,
    Thou canst not ioy long lacke.

Though gripes, and greefes full sore 5

Doe lodge with thee all night
Yet ioy and grace, shal be at hand
Ere that the day be light.

The Lord is kind and meeke 6
 When we doe make him greeue;
He is full slowe his wrath to shew,
 Great grace he doth vs giue.

And loe what loue good men 7
 To their owne seede doe beare.
Like grace the Lord doth shewe to such
 As searue him in his feare.

III. Sighe.

O that I had wings like a doue—my sweete Loue—that I might fly hence to thee, and so be at rest both in mind, in thought, in hart, in soule, and in mine whole.

THE FOURTH STRAINE.

THE Lord that made me knowes 1
 My shape, my mould, my lust:
 Howe weake, howe vaine, howe fraile,
  howe fond,
 And that I am but dust.

O God in me set vp 2
    A pure hart in thy sight;
And eke in all my parts let be
    A good and meeke sweete spright.

With thy sweete spright of power 3
    Cure thou O Lord my sore;
And I shall teach the good and ill
    To bowe to thy sweete lore.

My soule doth pant and bray, 4
    Mine hart is neere at rest,
But seekes to knowe thy lawe, thy will,
    And what may please thee best.

O would it might thee please 5
    My waies to set in right,
That I might both in hart and deed.
    Thy lawes to keepe in sight.

O Lord I doe tend still 6
    My daies, my time to serue,
That I nor mīe may haue a thought
    From thy lawes once to swerue.

O saue me then O God, 7
    Looke on me with thy health :
For that I rate at such a price
    More thē the wide world's wealth

IV. Sighe.

O let the words of my mouth, the thoughts of my hart, the tune of my voice, and touch of my tongue, be euer in thy sight O Lord as a sweet smell, for Christ, his sake, both at morne, eue, and none daye.

THE FIFT STRAINE.

WITH ioy Lord of the iust 1
   Let my poore soule be fraught:
That I may liue in peace and glee,
   And free from all that's naught.

Lord keepe me, for in thee 2
   I stay, and stand and feed:
Thou art my God, and of my goods
   O Lord thou hast noe need.

I giue them to the sainets 3
   That in the world doe dwell:
Yea to the folke of faith and loue,
   Whose care is to doe well.

My hart is prest for aye, 4
   And eke my tongue is soe:
I will raise vp my soule in song
   In spight of hell and foe.

To praise my God that hath 5
    Shewd loue and life to me,
And made me scape both bloud and blowe,
    And so did sett me free.

O Lord what shall I pay 6
    To thee for this thy grace:
I vowe to thee, my selfe, my life,
    My loue, and all my race.

Grant Lord, I beg and pray 7
    In thee that we may rest:
So shall our soules sing to thy praise,
    And aye in thee be blest.

V. Sighe.

O my God, why art thou gone from me, and why dost thou hide thy sweete face from my prayer, for I seeke thee, and sue to thee, with all my hart, and that thou knowest full well.

THE SIXT STRAINE.

MY soule giue praise to God, 1
    My spright shall doe the same,
And all the parts of hart and mind,
    Shall praise for aye his name.

Giue thankes for all his gifts   2
    Shew soule thy selfe most kind;
And let not his good deeds to thee
    Once slipp out of thy mind.

He quitt thee of thy faults,   3
    He rid thy life from death:
His good, his grace doth waite on thee,
    His word doth giue thee breath

If thou wert brought to graue,   4
    And turnd to mould and dust,
Yet he will giue thee life in store,
    As he to thee is iust.

Teach me then Lord to knowe   5
    Thy lawe, thy loue, thy lore;
Thy workes, thy words, as signes and seales
    I'le lay them vp in store.

O day of ioy to me   6
    When I learnd first to knowe
Howe for to scape my selfe, my sinne,
    And hell that is soe lowe.

I giue mine all to thee,   7
    My bud, my branch, my fruite:
I beg of thee, O Lord, my God
    To grant to me my suite.

VI. Sighe.

O my God, to thy hands I giue my spright
thou hast binc a pledge for me and that to death,
O God.   Thou art the God both of my health,
life, and rest for aye.

THE SEUENTH STRAINE.

LORD, thou hast me tride,   1
 And day by day dost knowe
My thoughts, my words, my lookes, my
 deeds,
 My sighs, my groans, my woe.

My bones they are not hid,   2
 Thou knewst them all, each one:
For in thy note they were all wrote
 Each ioynt, and bone by bone.

Trie still, and search mine hart,   3
 My thoughts proue day and night
And if the ill doe touch me Lord,
 O leade me to the right.

For thou canst rule my raines   4
 As when I was in wombe;
O giude me in this life of mine,
 And rest me in my tombe.

> Keepe me from men that muse 5
>   Of bloud of bane, of ill;
> O let me thinke of thee O Lord,
>   And howe to doe thy will.
>
> So shall noe shame me taynt 6
>   My corps, my goods, my name:
> So shall I rest in ioy and peace,
>   And touch noe blot of shame.
>
> So shall thy folke for me, 7
>   Be glad, and sing thy praise;
> So shall my selfe, my seed, my soule,
>   Be thine in all my daies.

VII. Sighe.

O let not my suite come in vaine to thee, but heare O my God, and say to my soule I am, and will be thy passe from hell, thy port from the sea of this world, and will bring thee to the bay of blisse.[1]

---

[1] Following this are two blank leaves or four pages, with border lines. G.

A months minde.

To Thinke on death, & muse
on the graue, that tho feare of death
may not bo fierce when Christ shall
call vs out of this world, & is to
bo song in the tune
of
I sayd I will looke to my waie.
PSALM. XXXIX.
*O death I will be thy death (saith
Christ) for he is the death of death, the
death of sinne, the life of man and the
breath of god for man to liue
there in world with
out end.*

HAMBOROUGH. Januarii 24.
1620.[1]

---

[1] Blank on reverse. G.

To [his much-respected good frend, Mr. THOMAS BARKER, one of the assistants of the worthy cōpanie of the Marchants Aduenturers, residing at Hamborough.

The blessing of both worlds in Christ Iesus.

WELBELOUED, There is nothing more comfortable to a spirituall minded mā then to muse and meditate of his departure hence into the blessed sight of Christ, in the other life: yet to a worldling that would build vp a rest for his body here, and sing a requiem to his soule in this vale of teares, nothing is more fearefull and hiddeous then for him to heare death spoken of. We must therefore examine our selues, whether we can sing a song of Siō in this exile and banishmēt, whether we can solace our selues, in hymnes and songs, of our ends and departure hence: For we must hence: nothing more sure; but the tyme when, the place where, and the manner how, nothing more vnsure. It is sufficient that God telleth vs, our life is but a flower that fadeth, an hower that passeth, a shadow that departeth, a vanity that vexeth, a momēt that warneth, a nothing when we haue done all we can. For our thoughts, our faults, our purposes, our proiects, our loues, our 'liues, when our breath departeth, perisheth in the twinckling of an eie. O then let vs meditate and muse to our selues, and sing and say to our soules, that our end and the last things, are not the least but the best things that we can consider of to mortifie vs and make vs meete for the sauing mercies of God in Christ; to which I recomend you in my dearest loue, and rest.

    Yours in life and death,
           W. Loe.

THE FIRST MUSE.

DEARE soule thou hast thought of thy 1
    end
    And nowe muse on the way ;
The first part is a life well spent,
    The last is death's doome's day.

Shall I call that the way of woe 2
    By which we passe to blisse ?
O sure there is noe way but that
    To bring me where Christ is.

And what is death nowe dost thou thinke 3
    But downe with all the stickes,
Of which this earth and tent of ours
    Is made, that gainst God kickes.

Death is the farewell of old frends, 4
    Till they meete to be blest;
Death is the iudge to quitt fñ iayle,
    The soule that longs for rest.

Death makes the corps of clay to sleepe, 5
    But wakes the soule to see ;

Death payes the debte and teares the bond,
And all to sett thee free.

There is a death of deaths my soule   6
    The death of hell and woe ;
But Christ, his death, hath payd for that ;
    His word doth tell thee soe.

O Christ, my soule doth thinke on thee,   7
    And thankes thee day and night,
That thou hast rid me frō this death,
    By thy great power and might.

I. Thought.

Thy Christ, O soule, hath set them free, who through feare of death were all their life time in bonds and thrall.
         Heb. 2. 15.

THE SECOND MUSE.

MUSE my soule, sith thou art safe,   1
    Get home ene to thy rest ;
For God to praise in songs and psalmes,
    I hold it for the best.

My soule, howe canst thou feare to goe   2
    In stepps where Christ hath bine ;

He hath to graue led thee the way
 O then leaue of to sinne.

For hire of sinne is death, and graue   3
 To death are deepe fell wayes;
There needs no kinues¹, noe cords, noe swords,
 It comes on nights and dayes.

One by a slatt,² a flye, a grape,   4
 One by a bit of meate:
One by the ayre, a flower, a thorne,
 Comes to his doome so great.

Why then my soule, feare not this death: 5
 The sting of it is lost:
The bed of graue is sweete, and safe
 Through Christ, his care and cost.

Our sinne made death our foe at last,   6
 Our frend Christ hath it made;
By death we pass the port of rest,
 When all things else doe fade.

What if this giude³ doe lead my corps   7
 Through graue both dark and fell?

---

[1] = knives. G.
[2] = slate or stone (falling from a roof). G.
[3] = guide, as before, and so throughout. G.

Whiles at that tyme my soule doth liue
And with my Christ doth dwell.

II. Thought.

O my soule, ioy and be glad, for thy Christ hath made thee say to death, O death where is thy death? O graue where is thy power?
1 Cor. 15, 55.

THE THIRD MUSE.

WHAT if my frends doe mourne for me 1
    And sobb and sighe in moane ;
What if my seed doe cry and roare,
    And greeue, and waile, and grone.

This while my soule sees him that was 2
    Once dead but nowe doth liue,
And that for aye my Christ in God,
    My Lord that life doth giue.

What care I who doth shutt mine eies, 3
    Whō death doth make me see
As I am seene of God in Christ,
    And then with him shall be.

What if my life the world doe not 4
    Set out in words of fame!

Whiles I liue with the God of life,
  What care I for the same.

If death showld still be foe to me,   5
  He harmes but my worst part;
My best part farre out of his reach
  Scornes both his ruth and dart.

And more then this, my corps once dead,   6
  Feeles noe more sting of death;
But then my soule is free, and liues
  In God, by Christ, his breath.

Nowe then my soule sith thou dost beare   7
  Two things wrapt vp in breast,
Lett each part turne, and goe, and see
  His seate, his scite, his rest.

III. Thought.

O God they that dwelt in a darke place, by thee haue seene the light, and they that walkt in the shade of death thou hast brought them to the light with great ioy and peace.

Esay. 9. 2.

THE FOURTH MUSE.

SHRINKE not deare soule at the sight of
 death   1
 Nor faint thou at God's call;
Howe oft hast thou hard bells to passe
 For frends, for foes, for all.

Howe oft hast thou the sicke bed sene,   2
 Of wights in woe most rife!
Howe oft haue things bine done to death
 And all to giue thee life.

And canst thou hope that some way else   3
 For thee is made in sence?
Whē kings, and prests, and rich, and poore
 And all must thus goe hence.

Passe on my soule, and sing, and ioy   4
 In God that makes the graue,
A place for thee to pass to blisse
 And knowes what thou wouldst haue.

Howe oft hast thou scene eies fast closd   5
 And heard by dint of sword,
Howe oft vaine men in field haue fought
 In fence of a vaine word.

What thē nowe dost thou feare my soule?   6
 The stage of death is bed,

And graue, that rests our bones in peace
    That here on earth haue fed.

Let them feare death whose hart and mind   7
    Is more sicke thē their face :
Howe canst thou feare since nowe thy Christ
    Hath shed his bloud for grace ?

IV. Thought.

O giue me light that am set in a dark place, and shade of death, and giude me by thy good grace O Christ, to the way of peace.
Luck. 1. 79.

THE FIFT MUSE.

WHAT losse is this sweet soule to loose   1
    This corps, this flesh, this skinn ?
When thou shalt winn thy God in Christ,
    Thy selfe fre'd from thy sinn.

When thou shalt see the soules, the saincts   2
    In ioy, in rest, in blisse :
Whē thou this world a sea of sinne
    A sinke, a stye, shalt misse ?

O change most blest for thee to knowe   3
    To rid thee of these raggs;
And thy selfe clad in robes of state
    In spight of death, his brags.

This skin, this shame, this dust, this dung,   4
    This earth, this mire, this clay,
Shall shine as sunne in raies of rest
    When thou shalt see that day.

Thine eies that were full sad to see   5
    Thine oft and ill done deeds;
Shall then see Christ still in thy sight
    Where grace and good still feeds.

These cares that heare the ruth and rage   6
    Of tongue, as hott as hell;
Shall then the voice of Christ still heare,
    And sainets, with him that dwell.

And thō this tongue that now doth plaine   7
    Of greefe, of woe, of gall,
Shall tune a part in that sweet quire
    With Christ, with sainets, with all.

V. Thought.

O my soule thy Christ hath tooke part with flesh and bloud, that by death he might beate downe him that had the power of death.

HEB. 2. 14.

THE SIXT MUSE.

NOWE what is death thē say my soule,   1
    I'st not a sleepe in graue?
  They that did feele the worst of it,
    The stile of sleepe it gaue.

And aske thy corps, O my sweete soule,   2
    Whē full with toyle of day,
If it hath not bine glad to rest
    As cloyd with a foule way.

And nowe in this sweete sleepe of death   3
    Thou art sure to be blest,
Why like a child wilt thou not goe
    To this thy bed, thy rest?

Didst thou ere see a bird in cage,   4
    Sitt still within the grate?
That might flie foorth to woods, to groues,
    To meete his loue, his mate?

Did Paule when God his gyues had burst 5
    And rid him out of iayle?
Crie out and say, not yet O Lord
    I doe not like this bayle.

Paule slepte twixt two that did him keepe 6
    But whē that he was free
And rid frō iayle, did he once turne
    To iayle those bonds to see?

O my sweete soule did'st ere thou see 7
    At sea, men sing their songs:
And whē to lād they cāe did greeue
    And tell their frends of wrongs?

VI. Thought.

O heare me O Lord, my God, and giue light to mine eies least I sleepe the sleepe of death.
Psal. 30. 3.

THE SEUENTH MUSE.

HAST thou O soule, no mind to rest 1
    In all thy paine and toyle?
But wilt thou still goe on and drudge
    By lott on sea, on soyle.

Howe oft haue wights in woe and greefe 2
  Sought death to ease their paine !
Hath death found thee, and wilt thou not
  To goe from greefe be faine ?

Doth name of death the[e] fright my soule ? 3
  What if mē call sleepe death,
Wilt thou be fraid to close thine eies
  Or feare to loose thy breath ?

What hurt will cōe to thee by that ? 4
  The first man was in sleepe
Whē God a wife made him for helpe,
  The man in ioy to keepe.

And what if nowe thy God for thee, 5
  Whilst thou dost sleepe in graue,
Doth make thy soule a spouse to Christ
  His face, his grace to haue ?

My death, O soule, but parts the frēds 6
  That each hath led the way,
And nowe shake hands but for a space
  Till meete in rest they may.

Goe then, my soule, to this sure gaine 7
  Part with a frend a space :
The tyme will come when this my dust,
  Shall see thy Christ, his face.

VII. Thought.

The due of sinne, my soule, is death, and graue, and hell: but the gift of God is life, ioy, and blisse, by Christ my Lord and God.
Rom. 6. 13.

THE EIGHT MUSE.

TELL me my soule was thou not loth 1
    At first to ioyne with me?
Why nowe art loth to part with that,
    Which much woe letts thee see.

Dost thou not heare the wise to say 2
    The day of death is cheefe;
And is more good then day of birth
    Which brings thee woe and greefe?

Dost thou not trust the wise man's words 3
    On throne, in state, in glee,
That thus did say of death and birth?
    Then hark thou once to me.

The Lord of life that knewe death's force 4
    Doth say that they are blest
That die in God, our Lord, our Christ
    And from their woes haue rest.

O death howe sweete is that thy rest 5
    To wights in vale of teares!
Howe sweete is thy grim face to those
    That liue in woe and feares!

O soule what man is so fell mad, 6
    And so in soule cast downe,
To hide himselfe in base things here
    To loose by them a crowne?

My soule then see and say in fine 7
    With men of God's owne lore;
For me to die it is more good
    Then liue on this ville shore.

VIII. Thought.

O, my soule, if by one man's sinne death did raigne by one, much more they which haue much grace and the gift of faith, shall raigne in life by one Christ, my Lord and God.

                        Rom. 5. 17.

THE NINGTH[1] MUSE.

WHAT ayles thee O my soule, my deare,   1
    Such face, such feare to shewe?
Nowe death doe come to cite thee home
  Is all thy faith, but dewe?

Is death soe fearce, so fell, to eies,   2
    To thoughts, that was soe free?
It is a shame to thee my soule,
    Thou dost noe more Christ see.

Where is thy faith? in words thou could'st   3
    Call oft for death, in life:
Is all but talke? is all but smoke?
    Where is thy hope so rife?

Hath thy sweete Christ now sent for thee   4
    And art thou loth to goe?
Rouze vp thy selfe for shame, O soule
    And doe not serue him soe.

O Lord, raise vp this hart of mine   5
    That faints and droopes in death!
O that I might thy cup once tast,
    And liue in thy sweete breath.

---

[1] Misprinted, ' nigth'. G.

The spright would come, but flesh is weake 6
  Lord helpe this guest of thine!
And rid her from this flesh of sinne
  Which is a broode of mine.

I come to thee, O Lord I come, 7
  Streach forth thine hand to me!
O death, O graue where is thy sting?
  My crowne, my God I see.

IX. Thought.

They are blest that haue a part in the first life: for on such, the last death shall haue noe strength, but they shal be preests of God, and of Christ.
                      Apoc. 20. 6.

Finis.

Alls Paulls Prayers.

Metaphrased into words of
one syllable of great Brittains
language, & are to be vsed by a devout
Christian soule in his priuate soliloquies,
& holy solaces with his
God.

*And are set to the tune of
I loue the lord because my voice.*
PSALM CXVI.

*O lord my god thou hast brought
vp my soule from out of the graue & thou
didst hold me from those that goe
downe to the pitt.*

To his much esteemed good frend Mr. NICHOLAS BACKHOUSE marchant, one of the assistants of the worthy companie of the Marchant Aduenturers residing at Hamborough.

The ioy of Ierusalem, and peace of Syon.

MUCH endeered, The cheefest parts of God's seruice, are either prayer or praise: prayer for what we want: praise in thanksgiuing for what we haue receaued.

The sweete singer of Israell in his heauenly composed hymes vseth both to pray to God and to praise God. I need not recomend vnto you prayer. I hope you vse it; as I knowe you doe publikely soe I doubte not but you vse it also priuately. Preaching is God's speach to you: prayer is ours to him. Preaching belongs to me; I preach to you as your pastor, and pray for you also. Prayer belongs to you, to pray for me, your selfe, all yours, all God's childrē. For the manner howe noe better president, noe more perfecte patterne, then S. Paull's practice in his prayers, which I haue here metaphrased for you in the syllables of your owne mother-tongue. God the father is the obiecte of your prayers and prayses. God the Sonne the presenter of them, as the only Master of Bequests in heauen. God the Holy Ghost the very breath of your prayers, the smile[1] of your soule. Vse this blessed exercise both of prayer and praise. Be in loue with it, and God will loue you. To which loue of his in this modell of my best loue to you, I recomend your well disposed thoughts in the sauing mercies of Christ Iesus your Lord and mine. Resting,

To be required by you, or your frends in Christ's seruice.

W. Loe.

---

[1] Misprinted 'simle' here and so in next piece. G.

THE FIRST PRAYER.

CEASE not to giue thankes to thee,   1
   O God, my God most iust,
For all thy gifts of grace and loue,
   To vs that liue in dust.

And Lord I craue a glympse of light   2
   In Christ my Lord, thy sonne.
That so my faith may see that sight,
   And to it still may runne.

That I may knowe thy becke, thy call,   3
   My hope, my helpe, my all:
That I may haue thy power and strength,
   To helpe me when I fall.

For thou O God, hast made vs see   4
   What thou hast wrought in loue:
For thy sweete spouse thy Church, thy wife,
   Thy ioy, thy smile, thy doue.

For thou hast set our Christ, O God,   5
   At thy right hand to shine:
And thou to that place wilt vs bring
   For that deare loue of thine.

O God, thou laidst my Christ full lowe   6
    Within the earth so darke:
But thou didst raise him vp on high
    And settst him as a marke.

On which we fix our eies of faith   7
    Our harts, our minds, our loue:
O bring vs all to him, sweete God,
    That is our deere, our doue.

O God, my hart is fixt on thee, and my tongue shall sing, and giue praise to thy name for aye.
Psal. 108. 1.

THE SECOND PRAYER.

DAY by day doe bowe to thee
    And cease not in the night
To seeke thee, Lord, in all my thoughts
    And muse of all thy might.

For of our Christ is made[1] the churc.   2
    Of vs that liue in clay,
And eke thy guard[2] and saincts on high
    That praise thee day by day.

---

[1] Misprinted 'nāde'. G.
[2] Misprinted 'gaurd'. G.

Grant vs, O Lord, that we may knowe 3
  Thy grace, our good, our end:
And that we may feele power and strength,
  And Christ may be our frend.

Let him dwell in our harts, O Lord, 4
  And then we shall thee see,
With all thy sainets in breadth and length
  In depth, in height, in glee.

Then shall we knowe the loue of Christ 5
  That else is past our skill,
The shalt thou fill vs with thy grace,
  In him to doe thy will.

O Lord for vs this thou can'st doe 6
  And more then all, that is
Of thy good grace to worke in vs,
  In Christ how should we misse.

Praise be to thee in all the world, 7
  Thy church doe sing the same,
And age to age shall eke sett forth
  For aye, to ours, thy name.

O God thou art my God, ere it be day will I seeke thee: my soule and flesh doe thirst and long for thee, as drie land which wants raine.

PSAL. 63. 1.

THE THIRD PRAEYR.

Phillippians I. 9.

GRAUNT to vs Lord that loue may dwell 1
 In these poore tents of ours;
For we must hence we knowe full [well],[1]
 And fade as doe the flowers.

And graūt good Lord that in thy loue   2
 It may growe more and more,
That we may knowe what things are ill
 And lead not to thy loue.

So may we in the day of doome   3
 In Christ be void of shame,
And fild with his faire fruits of loue
 May scape the rod of blame.

Then shall we sing the praise to thee   4
 In midst of all thy sainets,
Then shall our soule[2] be glad, and ioy,
 That nowe is weake, and faints.

I cease not Lord to pray for those   5
 That seeke and sue to thee,
That they may knowe howe safe and sure
 In Christ their soules may be.

---

[1] 'Well', as inadvertently dropped, supplied by us. G.
[2] Misprinted 'soules'. G.

And that we all may walke and worke   6
    In word, in worth, in all,
As he that hath vs cald to this,
    And rid vs of our thrall.

Who hath vs fre'd from power of death   7
    Frō foggs and doggs of hell :
And set vs by his chaire of state,
    With Christ for aye to dwell.

Saue vs, O Lord our God, and bring vs from those that doe not call on thee, that we may call on thee, and laud and praise thy name for aye.
PSAL. 106. 47.

THE FOURTH PRAYER.
THESSALONIANS III. 11.

THE Lord our God, our strength and stay   1
    Make vs to loue each one ;
And make vs knowe howe that we are
    Made all of flesh and bone.

That soe we may growe vp in grace   2
    And firme in hart and minde :
That soe to all we may set forth
    Our loue both sure and kind.

Yea not to cease till that our Lord   3
   Doe come in clouds full bright,
To iudge this earth, and all the folke,
   Yea all the world, in sight.

For is it not the loue of Christ   4
   Who did loue vs so deare,
That we through hope of grace in him
   Should liue voyd of base feare.

Lord be thou ioy to all our harts!   5
   Our words, our workes good make,
That we may loue and liue in thee,
   For thy sonne Christ, his sake.

O God of peace, of loue, of life   6
   Grant vs to serue thee still
In spright, in soule, in hart, in mind
   And this of thy good will.

Yea keepe vs Lord frō blame and blott   7
   Till Christ doth come in skey :
So shall we sure be of thy loue,
   To liue, when we shall die.

Heare me O Lord, and that soone, for my soule doth waxe faint: hide not thy face from me, least I be like them that goe downe to the graue.

            Psal. 148. 7.

THE FIFT PRAYER.

Romans. VII. 25.

THANKE thee Lord, that hast sett nowe 1
   In me a fight, a iarre;
My mind, my flesh, doe day by day
   In strife sett forth a warre.

My mind to thy sweete lawe giues way,   2
   My flesh in thrall is brought;
My mind would keep thy lawe, thy lore,
   And hath thy will still sought.

But my base flesh is prompt, and seekes   3
   Thy lawe to cast me fro.
O God what shall I doe in this?
   With me the case is so.

My mind would doe the good full faine,   4
   That thy lawes shewe to me,
But still my flesh doth frett and fume
   Gainst this thy lawe to me.

For I doe not that which I loue   5
   But I doe that I hate,
And all for that my mind is vext
   With this my flesh, my mate.

What shall I doe O Lord my God   6

Ah wretch who setts thee free?
Fis this fell death of sinne and shame
   That I thy grace may see.

I thanke my God who haue me fre'd
   For his sonne Christ, his sake;
To him for aye both night and day,
   My hymnes, my songs I make.

O God that thou wouldst beat downe the strong and ill man, that rules and raignes in my weake flesh, that I may say to him goe farre from me.
    Psal. 139. 19.

THE SIXT PRAYER.

Romans. xvi. 24.

THE grace of God be all my giude.   1
   His power be all my staye,
   His strength eke be to me a staffe,
By night, and eke by day.

For he it is that hath me taught   2
   That which the world nere knewe,
Till Christ our Lord was made to vs
   Our Lord, our God in vewe.

To God in hymnes, still will I sing,   3
    His praise in all my mirth :
The world shall sett him forth in praise.
    In all parts of the earth.

If there be wight that liues in life,   4
    And doth not loue our God,
Let him tast of the Lord of hosts
    His curse, his wrath, his rod.

But let the loue of God, and grace   5
    Of Christ, be with you all
That loue and looke, and long for him,
    To rid vs of our thrall.

And let our God that brought from death   6
    Our Christ, our grace, our blisse,
Set vs with sainets in ioy, in light
    Where as our Christ nowe is.

So shall we tūe[1] in that sweete quire   7
    Midst of those sainets in rest ;
And see his sainets in light of lights,
    And so for aye be blest.

O God let them that hate thee flie from thy sight

---

[1] = Tune. G.

mist doth from the sunne, but let them
that oue thee be glad and ioy in thee.

Psal. 68. 1.

THE SEUENTH PRAYER.

Hebrews. xiii. 20.

 GOD we are poore sheepe that stray   1
    In woods, in waies of sinne :
Bowe downe thine eare to vs, and heare
    And rid vs of this dinne.

That we may knowe thy grace in Christ   2
    That keepes vs as his flocke,
That leads vs forth to streames of ioy,
    And setts vs on a rocke.

That soe we may ore see this world   3
    And all the things in it :
And then doe place vs vp on high
    With him in ioy to sit.

Graũt vs good Lord that we may see   4
    The good that doth thee please :
So shall we liue in hart, in mind
    In ioy, in rest, in ease.

Graunt Lord what thou dost bid vs doe   5
    That we may doe the same :

Bid what thou wilt and graūt vs grace
And we will praise thy name.

To Christ our Lord the Lambe of God   6
That shed his bloud for sinnes,
To rid vs from the feends of hell
And all their crafts and ginns.

Be praisd of vs all tymes and tyds
In woe, and eke in wealth :
And let the folke on all the earth
Giue laud to him for health.

O Lord God of our health, I crie day and night to thee, let my grones come nigh to thee, and bowe downe thine eare to my sighes, that I make to thee.[1]

---

[1] Following this again are two blank leaves, with border lines, and after next title-page, one blank page.   G.

The song of songs

Or the Canticle of Solomon
betweene Christ & his spouse,
the two first chapters, & is set to
the tune of
Blessed are they that perfect are.
PSAL. CXIX. 1 part.

To his much esteemed good freend Mr. WILLIAM CHRISTMAS, Marchant, one of the deacons of the English Church residing at Hamborough:

Grace here, glory for euer in Christ.

LOUING, and beloued frend, the title of this heauenly hymne sheweth the excellency thereof. For it is called the song of songs, or the Canticles of wise Soloman. The subiecte is most sacred, for it is the nuptiall louesong betweene Christ and his Spouse. Wherein their mutuall loues by sweete resēblāces are mystically and maruelously expressed. What more comfortable song then to sing our hart's loue we beare to Christ, in the blessed vnion by one spirit, wherby we haue euerlasting life. Two of the first chapters of which song I haue metaphrased into monosyllables, which I haue bequethed to your loue as a signe of mine, and to seale both ours. Receaue it as the rest of your colleagues, for I wish you all the happines of both worlds in the sauing mercies of Christ, to which I recommend you and all that looke vpon you with loue, resting,

    Yours because of Christ,

        W. Loe.[1]

[1] Following this is a blank leaf, as before. G.

THE FIRST SONG.

The Spouse speakes to Christ.

O THAT thou wouldst on me so cast   1
  Some lookes of thy sweete loue,
That thou maist make me deere to thee
  My hart with grace to moue.

Thy loue O Christ is farre more deare,   2
  And farre more sweete to me
Then wealth, or wine, or limbe, or life,
  Or ought that I can see.

The sweete that I smell of thy name   3
  Is like an oyle most pure,
And pourd it is on all thy sainets,
  Such is thy loue soe sure.

O drawe me, drawe me, I will runne   4
  To bord, to bed, with thee ;
O pull me, pull me from my sinne,
  O rid me, set me free.

The good are glad in thee ; thy loue   5
  They long and looke for still :

They walke to thee, they talke of thee,
    And all to doe thy will.

Graunt this O Christ, and then we shall   6
    Be all in all that is,
And thou shalt find that none of vs
    Of thy grace ought to misse.

O shew me, whom my soule doth loue,   7
    Where thou dost feed at noone:
O why should I thus freet, and feele
    The losse of thee so soone.

THE SECOND SONG.
Christ speakes to his Spouse.

THOU my church, whom I doe loue   1
    For whō I shed my bloud,
If thou knowe not what thou dost craue,
    And hast not seene the good:

Then get thee to these flockes of mine   2
    Where as they feed by those
Whom I haue sett as giuds for them
    That I in loue haue chose.

There feed and fatt thy selfe with foode,   3
    That saincts doe touch, doe tast;

And tune their soules in thankes to me
  For loue that aye doth last.

For deere thou art to me my loue,   4
  For shape, for strength, for speede :
That none is like to thee my deere
  In thought, in word, in deede.

Those parts of thee where loue doth looke   5
  Are set with pearls of grace,
With stones of price, with chaynes of worth :
  I loue to see thy face.

These signes of loue, are scales to thee,   6
  What shall be thine else where,
When thou shalt shine in bliss with me
  O spouse, my loue most deere!

There spangs, and specks of gold most pure   7
  Ile add to all the rest :
There shalt thou loue, and liue with me
  And eke for aye be blest.

THE THIRD SONG.

The Spouse speakes to her mates.

EE nowe all ye that loue the Lord 1
    Ye nymphes, ye mayds of grace,
Whiles that my Lord and king nowe seemes
    Farre of from me in place.

And is in midst of troopes of sainctes 2
    On highe where he doth dwell ;
Where all doe tend on him in loue,
    Where all things sure goes well.

Yet see his grace doth stoope to me, 3
    I feele him with me here ;
By power of spright, by gifts of light,
    He comes to me most neere.

And though I be much ioy to him,
    Yet he is all to me ;
As bunch of myrrhe twixt both my breasts,
    So sweete to hart is he.

Oh is there ought in the wide world 5
    That smells, that smiles as he ?
Ah sweete, ah sweete, my soule doth feele
    His loue a life to me.

His loue layd close to my poore hart   6
  To sence giues such a touch,
That for his loue to dye, to dye,
  I would not thinke it much.

Watch then and wayte ye maids that mourne,
  For this my loue will come;
And iudge he will in truth, and power
  The folke, both all and some.[1]

THE FOURTH SONG.

Christ speakes to his Spouse.

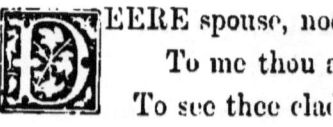EERE spouse, noe loue is lost on me,
  To me thou art most sweete:
To see thee clad in clothes of grace
  With rings, and roabs most meete.

I ioy, I like, I loue thee deere,   2
  Howe faire, how fresh art thou!
None like to thee in shine of face,
  As I looke on thee nowe.

Howe chast, howe choice art thou my deere! 3
  Thine eies like doues doe looke.

---

[1] = the race and the individual. G.

Thine hart, thy mind, thy thoughts, thy all,
I write thē in my booke.

The Spouse speakes to Christ.

Nay thou my deere, thou art the cheefe,   4
    The choice, the sunne, the shine !
From thee O Christ, I haue these raies,
    For they are none of mine.

Thou art O Christ, full of this grace,   5
    Thou art the sea, the spring ;
And from thee I doe take these streames
    And to thee thē doe bring

As thankes for all thy loue to me,   6
    And to thy saincts each one ;
Who troope in bands to serue thee still,
    Though here they weepe, and mone.

For they are sure to rest in blisse   7
    When thou shalt call them home
From out this sea of sobs and sighes
    That doth soe frett and fome.

THE FIFT SONG.

Christ speakes to his Spouse.

DEERE spouse, I am both faire and 1
    sweete :
  Of field I am the rose,
And sure all such as liue by me,
  Full choice I am to those.

All thinges else that this world hath, be 2
    Vile weeds, which are most base :
I am the sweet, the sence, the smell,
  That yeald them all the grace.

And thou O loue art mongst the maids 3
    All choice and cheefe in vewe :
Nought in the earth is like to thee.
  In face, in shine, in hue.

The Spouse speakes to Christ.

O thou my deare, that one I loue 4
    Thou art the tree of life ;
Thy shade let sheeld me from all harms
  And I will be thy wife.

Thou with thy spright shalt lead me forth 5
    To the sweete streames of good,

And I shall be fresht with thy loue,
 Wrought to me in thy bloud.

O stay me, stay me, take a care,   6
 O cheare my soule that faints;
O come for I am sicke of loue
 To liue in midst of sainets.

O put thy left hand to my head   7
 Thy right hand to my side!
O stay me vp both head and hart,
 And still be thou my guide.

THE SIXT SONG.

The Spouse speakes.

CHARGE ye O you soules of sainets,
 By roes and hindes of loue,
Take heed howe you doe vexe and greeue
 The spright of my sweete doue.

Take heed you wrong not his great name,   2
 With life soe leaud, so vaine,
And doe not dare to moue his ire,
 Who would saue you so fayne.

Loe I doe call, and he doth heare,   3
 And sends to me his voice;

My moūts of sinnes, and hills of shame
    Haue not soe lowd a noice.

Noe roe, noe hinde, soe swift cā rūne   4
    Nor make such speede as he :
When I doe call, or crie for him,
    He comes, he runnes to me.

The Spouse speakes.

And though this vaile of my base flesh   5
    A full sight bares me fro,
Yet with mine eye of faith, I looke
    On him that loues me soe.

I see him as in a cleare glasse,   6
    I see him shine full bright ;
Through grates of words and gates of life,
    My soule of him hath sight.

And nowe me thinkes I heare him speake   7
    And thus to me doth say :
O church, O spouse, lift vp thy head
    O faire one come thy way.

THE SEUENTH SONG.

Christ speakes.

THE storme is past of greefe and woe,   1
    The spring of ioy is seene:
And all things nowe are fresh and faire
    And full, and newe, and greene.

On highe is ioy, on earth is peace,   2
    To men a great good will;
And all the quire of sainets doe sing
    To shewe their loue, their skill.

Not buds, but figgs and fruits are seene   3
    Of grace, of ioy, of loue;
O come my deere, shake of thy sleepe,
    Come on my milke white doue.

O let me heare thy voice my deere   4
    O plye me with thy plaints,
O looke thou vp though face be sad
    Ile place thee with my sainets.

O all ye that wishe well to me,   5
    And to my church and name,
Put frō my deere all those that seeke
    Her faith, her loue to blame.

The Spouse speakes.

For he is mine by faith and trust.   6
    And I am his by loue.
We both are one by his great power:
    I long to see my doue.

O come as swift as roe or hind   7
    My loue, my life to me:
Till day doe breake, till sunne doe shine,
    Till shade of death doth flee.[1]

Following these are two blank leaves, as before, and so throughout between each piece and reverse of title-pages: not marked further. G.

A Canticle, or song.

Of the third & fourth chapters
of the song of Solomon being Metaphrased into Monosylables of Great Brittains
language, & is to be vsed by euery deuout
soule in his priuat confcrence
with his god.

And is set to the tune of
Helpe lord for good, & godly men.
PSAL. XII.

To his much esteemed good frend, Mr. ISAAC LEE, one of the assistants of the most worthy companie of the Marchant-Adventurers, residing at Hamb.

Encrease of Glory,

MORE thē much beloued, When God brought man forth at the first, he put him not into a wildernes, but into a garden, a paradise and place of pleasure. Wherby I see that his sacred maiestie did not reioyce in the misery, but in the delight and happines of his creatures. Cheerefulnes therefore pleaseth God better then dulnes, dumpishnes, and heauines of hart. Let vs be godly and good in our pleasures, and it will neuer displease our Maker; neither will he grudge or repine at our joy. To this purpose haue I framed certayne hymns for the priuat solace of such as shall take delight there in. One portion whereof I have consecrated to you. Let yt' haue acceptance of you by your practice of yt. I expect no other guerdon for my paines. For the Highest knowes with what an honest hart I composed this and the rest, and what a desire I had in the framing thereof for the good of many. I haue euer hated [that] Epicurean resolution: 'Let vs eate and drinke, to morrowe we shall dye'. But I haue euer loued entyrely [that] Christian exhortacion: 'Let vs pray, and praise God, to morrowe we shall liue'. For to loue, is to liue, and where we loue, there we liue. If we loue God, we shall liue in him by our prayers, by our prayses, and all by one Spirit. O then let vs so loue him, that we may liue in him in our daylie voices, that they may be hard to his glory, our comfort, and good example of our brethren. The God of heauen ioy your hart in all your life, and in your death, that we may all meete to sing together in the quire of heauen with the angells in the sauing mercies of our Sauiour Christ.

Yours much more then mine owne,

W. Loe.

THE FIRST SPEACH.

The Spouse speakes to Christ.

IN bed I sought my loue by night,   1
    But could not find him there,
  I sought him, but he was farre off,
    And did not come me neere.

I rose, and walkt the streates to see   2
    If my soule could him find
Whom I did want, yet found I not
    The day-starre of my mind.

Thē rā I straight to those that teach   3
    And watch and waite for me,
And sayd to thē, cā ye shewe nowe
    Where I my loue might see.

And thus halfe spent with care and cost,   4
    My soule gan faint and faile:
Loe then my loue did shewe himselfe:
    And would not let me quaile.

So that by a newe acte of faith   5
    I sawe where he was not.

We misse him in our beds of rest,
    The world is not his lott.

The streets are strayts of cost and care   6
    Where we doe lose him quite ;
But in the Word, and soule of man
    We feele him in his might.

But whē I found him, hold I tooke   7
    Fast hold on him I layd,
Noe more to part with him at all :
    Then he to me thus sayd.

THE SECOND SPEACH.

*Christ speake*s *to his Spouse.*

NOWE that my spouse hath toyld all night
    And lokt and longd for me,
I charge you all that are my frends,
    And looke to hue in glee.

Stirre her not vp, nor wake my deere   2
    With toyes, or tales of goe.
But let her rest in peace and ioy,
    And vexe her nowe noe more.

Oh who is this that comes so faire   3
    From out the foule world's lane,

And hath shakt of[f] her slough of sinne
That would haue beene her bane?

It is my Church, my chaire of state 4
  Where I doe loue to be:
It is my doue, my stay, my deere,
  It glads me her to see:

That is so quitt from world of woe, 5
  From sinke of siune and shame;
She seekes to me for all her wants,
  Shee trusts to my great name:

She smells as myrrh and spice of cost 6
  Graed with my chaines of loue;
She is my spouse, no spott she hath,
  She is my milke-whit doue.

All faire and full of grace most bright 7
  She comes, she rūns to me:
Come on my deere, make thou noe stay,
  Thy loue, thy life to see.

THE THIRD SPEACH.

The Spouse speakes.

NOWE my soule thou hast a glymse   1
    Of ioy that is on high!
O blest are they that vewe it all,
    Or doe that place come nighe.

The courts on earth of kings most greate   2
    Are rich and rare to vewe;
But this, where my Christ rules and raignes,
    For aye is fume and newe.

The gard of this great court of state   3
    Are sainets and sprightes of might,
That doe his will at all his beckes,
    And dwell with him in light.

The courts of kings are made with hands   4
    Their care, their cost is vaine;
But here's a Court not made by mē
    Where my sweete Christ doe raigne.

The Spouses speaketh. [sic]

He in him selfe is all the state,   5
    He giues his Court the grace;
He is the light, the hight, the all,
    That is still in that place.

Come forth ye saincts of God in Christ,   6
  And see this court of rayes :
O take a vewe of this your life,
  O seeke it all your dayes.

Christ is your Bride groome, and you are,   7
  To him a spouse most bright ;
He hath you bought with bloud most deere
  And gaynd you with his might.

THE FOURTH SPEACH.

Christ speakes to his Spouse.

HOWE faire art thou my deare, my spouse   1
  With out, and eke with in !
Howe voyd of filth or spotts of shame,
  Of sinke or stinch of sinne !

For I doe purge thee of the same,   2
  My word doth make thee free,
And they that teach to thee my lore
  Are all most sweet to thee.

Their speach is full of grace and loue,   3
  To those that heare the same ;
Their words are impt[1] with zeale of loue
  To keepe thee fr̄o all blame.

---

[1] An 'imp' is a graft or shoot inserted into a tree :

Those that doe rule and giude the stearne   4
 Are as the necke to head :
They are both strong and stout to gard
 The soules that they haue fed.

The two sweet bookes of league most newe   5
 Are breasts full fraught with milke,
And all that sucke the ioyes of thē
 Are clad in robes of silke.

That is the grace of saincts, and such
 Shall shine in rayes of rest :
Till day doth dawne, and shad[e] doth fade,
 And they for aye be blest.

Thus art thou faire, my loue in me,
 In thee there is noe spott :
I will in blisse sett thee my deere,
 Cleane voyd of sinne or blott

---

hence to 'engraft' and hence, as here, to add and so to strengthen. So SHAKESPEARE "imp out our drooping country's broken wings" (Richard II. ii. 1) and MILTON "her broken league to *imp* her serpent wings" (Sonnets X. 8.) These two quotations remind us that the term was originally used of the Falconer's repairing of the hawk's wing by adding feathers. G.

THE FIFT SPEACH.

Christ speakes still.

 NOWE my loue I haue thee sought,   1
   And brought thee frō the lands;
I haue the[e] led in bands of grace
   From out the curse and bands.

To me from all parts of the earth   2
   I will the[e] guide and call;
And quite¹ thou shalt be frō the bauds
   Of them that did thee thrall:

Who once did vexe and greeue thee sore,   3
   In bane, in bloud, in woe;
But I will saue thee safe from them,
   And rid thee from thy foe.

For thou my hart hast caught with loue,   4
   One cast of thy faire eie,
Of faith I meane, doth wound my hart,
   Which made me faint and die.

Christ speakes still.

All sweets the world can yeald to me   5
   Are banes to thy sweet smell;

---

¹ = quit, released. G.

Thou art my spouse, in life and death,
　The graue shall not thee quell.

The words which from thy lipps doe droppe 6
　When thou dost pray or praise,
Are farre more sweet to me then sweets
　That sunne doth see by dayes.

Thou art a spring to me shutt vp, 7
　A well seald by my ring :
Frō whēce doth flowe pure streames of loue,
　To me thy lord and king.

THE SIXT SPEACH.

Christ speakes.

THOU art closd vp my spouse, my deere 1
　That none might doe thee ill ;
　That force of foes, nor rage of fēds,[1]
　On thee might doe their will.

That noe wild boore of wood, so fell, 2
　Thy rootes, thy plants might marre :
For I looke on thee with mine eies,
　And vewe their ire a farre.

= fiends. G.

Thy plants are like sweet fruits of choice 3
  My deere ones all they are,
Of thee and them, as of mine eies
  I watch and haue a care.

Sweet sent as myrrhe and cane ye yeald, 4
  As all cheefe spice of choice:
So are thy plants O deere, to me,
  For they doe heare my voice.

For tast, for touch, for smell, for hewe, 5
  Thy fruits are all most pure,
I ioy to see them in this plight,
  And in my loue so sure.

From thee O spouse doth flowe full farre 6
  Thy streames to dales and hills,
And I the spring doe flowe to thee
  To fill thy spouts, thy rills.

Who so of thee doth drink is drencht, 7
  And thirsts no more for aie:
Thou art the streames of God, to flowe,
  To soules that faint in waye.

THE SEUENTH SPEACH.

The Church speakes to Christ.

IF I be then so sweet my deere 1
    My Christ, my God, my Loue,
The breathe on me with thy sweet breath,
    That it my hart may moue.

O all ye powers of my sweete God
    Blowe on me North and South,
That these my plants of my poore soule
    May blest be by his mouth.

And make the sweet to him, as are 3
    The plants of loue and grace :
So shall my loue ioy still to come,
    And glad him in this place.

Yea he will come to me, his owne 4
    Which he hath bought full deere,
And will take of the fruit that he
    Hath made to him so neere.

Christ speakes.

I come my loue to thee, myne own 5
    As thou hast cald to me :
And as thou wilt, so will I take
    These fruits, a part of thee.

I see thy workes, thy words, thy thoughts 6
    They all to me are sweet,
For they are mine, I gaue thē thee,
    And all else that is meete.

Nowe all ye blest of me, and saincts 7
    Cheere vp and glad your mind,
That yett in this deere loue of mine
    Such grace and loue doe find.

A Canticle, or song

Betweene Christ, & his church
of the fift, and sixt chapters of the Song of
Solomon, metaphrased into Monosyl-
labls of Great Brittains language, & is to
be vsed by every deuout soule in his
priuat conference with
his god.

And is set to the tune of
Lord be my iudge, and thou shalt see.
PSAL. CXXVI.

To his much esteemed good frend Mr. WALTER PELL, one of the assistants of the most worthy cōpanie of the marchants-Adventurers, residing at Hamb :

Ioy of both worlds,

LOUING frend, If you would die well, you must endeuour to liue well. Then let your death be neuer so suddaine, it will not come vnexpected, neither will you be vnprepared. The daies and houers of daies that you haue spent in Gods seruice, either in praying or praysing him shalbe so many cordialls of comforts and consciences of well led purposes, and will so take vp your hart in ioye and solace, that noe terrour of death, or darkenes shall appale yt. Who would not then be busie in this so serious, so sacred a busines? Let vs neuer thinke to be soundly merry, if this be not our musique. Reason and Religion guides vs here vnto. For veary Reason sheweth vnto vs that we must all die, and Religion enlighteneth vs howe we may die well. Fooles iudge actions by euents, but the wise forsee by iudgmēt of reason and faith, what will inevitably ensue. To this purpose all this is sayd, that as I haue in myne endeered loue, sent you an introduction herevnto in this paper-token, so you would accept and practize it. So shall I euer rest your votary, praying to God for your eternal happines in Christ Iesus, his sauing mercies.

Your perpetuall votary,

W. LOE.

THE FIRST SPEACH.

Christ speakes to his Spouse.

AM come downe O spouse most deere, 1
    To take those fruites of thine,
Which thou with hart and grace of loue,
    Dost knowe of erst were mine.

I haue thought well of all thy workes, 2
    As well of will as deede.
I dranke thy wine with millke so sweet,
    With loue they doe me feede.

O you my freds and saincts most blest, 3
    Cheere vp yourselues with me,
And ioy your harts with this my spouse,
    Whose cates of love you see.

The Church speakes.

When once this world had luld in sleepe 4
    Of sinne, my selfe, my sēce,
Yet wakt mine hart to Christ my Deere,
    And thou didst drawe me thence.

Christ speakes to his Spouse.

Thou camst to me, and knockst full oft 5
    At doore of my poore hart :
Thou knockst I say full oft my deere,
    And pearst me with thy dart.

And saidst Ile come and lodge with thee, 6
    And dwell with thee in grace.
Shut out the world, thy sinns, thy shame,
    And let me come in place.

For all the night I wayte for thee, 7
    My lockes with dropps of paine
Are wett, and all to stay for thee
    That I thy loue might gaine.

THE SECOND SPEACH.

The Church speakes.

I HAUE put of my coate sayd I, 1
    Howe shall I put it on ?
My feete I washt, shall I them file ?
Oh noe, my loue be gone.

Thus did I plead for my long stay : 2
    For who so loues my deere

Must care, and carke, and strangle things
  tast,
 Of woe, him to come neere.

For cleane of soyle, of woe and ill 3
  Who liues that seekes my deere?
No, no, the world will plague th͠ all
  That serues our God in feare.

But wh͠ my loue these words did heare 4
  He shrunke, and went me fro,
And hid him selfe, and spake noe more
  That I had scarud him so.

And then I rouzd my hart, I yearnd 5
  That had him lost so sone:
I rose, and lokt, and chid my selfe
  For that which I had done.

I sought him, but he hid him selfe, 6
  And would not me come nigh:
I roard and cride, and vsd all meanes,
  I card not for to die.

For that I had lost him my deere 7
  That sought me for his doue,
But yet I foūd him not, nor knewe
  He hard my voice in loue.

THE THIRD SPEACH.

The Church speakes still.

HE men that should haue had a care 1
 They smote, and did me wound ;
With words most false and vaine, they
  sought,
 To ding¹ me to the ground.

I charge you all that loue the Lord 2
 If that you shall him find,
Tell him howe sicke I am of loue
 In hart, in soule, in mind.

O what—say they—is this thy deere 3
 More then the sonnes of men
That thou art thus farre gō in loue,
 And aye doe not him ken?

My loue sayd I is white and red, 4
 His face is pure and bright:
He is the cheefe and choice of all,
 In him is all the light.

For God in him is full and faire, 5
 In grace, in face, in all.

---

¹ A living wo[r]d in Scotland still = cast. G.

His head fine gold, his lockes faire flockes,
   In him there is no gall.

His eies like doues, full of pure loue   6
   His cheeks are beds of spice;
His lips are sweet as flowers in May,
   To me he is most¹ nice.

His ha'ds are sett with port² and price,   7
   Pure myrrhe doth dropp him fro:
His will is rule of truth and faith:
   This is most true I knowe.

THE FOURTH SPEACH.

The Spouses speaketh. [*sic*]

EA all his acts are firme and strong   1
   As sett in gold most sure:
No shewe of change, but streight and
      cleere
   Both sound, and safe, and pure.

---

¹ Misprinted 'not'. G.

² port = state or splendor. So Shakespeare, Taming of the Shrew (i. 1)
   " Thou shalt be master, Tranio in my stead:
   Keep house, and *port*, and servants as I should ":
et alibi. See onward for 'port' again. G.

His mouth is as sweet things of choice, 2
    Frō whēce doth flowe my blysse :
He is all sweet, in part, in whole,
    And I poore soule am his.

A forraigne congregatio speakes.

Since then O deere such is thy loue, 3
    Shewe vs where he is found,
And we will seeke this loue with thee,
    In all the world so round.

For nōe, but thee O church cā'st him 4
    Make knowne, in word, in deed :
O tell vs then, and we will ioyne,
    And he shall be our meede.

Thē sayd I to those that him sought 5
    He is gone downe to be
In beds of spice, with soules and sainets:
    That is my loue, that's he.

Yea I am his in his sweet loue, 6
    And he is mine by faith :
In spight of hell, or sinne, or shame
    His word to me so saith.

And both of vs are one in God,
    And knitt in soule and spright.   7
By loue most sweete and ioy of hart
    I liue still in his sight.

THE FIFT SPEACH.

Christ speakes to his Church.

THOU thou my Church did'st me not seeke,   1
    But putts me farre thee fro,
Yet nowe thou dost looke back to me,
    I will not serue thee so.

But I will come and dwell with thee   2
    In grace, in loue, in awe.
I will thee ioy, in mirth and glee,
    And teach to thee my lawe.

Turne backe thine eies frō me my deere   3
    That art thus fixt on me,
Thy strength of faith doth ioy me so,
    That I mind none but thee.

The men that feede thy soule with foode   4
    Haue all one hart, one tongue,
They tune all like a quire of sainets,
    They sound forth all one songe.

So that their paines are not in vaine,   5
  They bring to me much fruit:
They cry and call to me for helpe,
  And I doe heare their suite.

Thy locks, thy lookes, are seene so faire   6
  Thy blush, thy smile so sweet,
That I doe ioy in them that teach
  Those things that are so meete.

Though kings and queens, and all folk else   7
  My name and loue doe vse,
Yet on thee, on thee loue, I looke,
  On thee, I thinke, I muse.

THE SIXT SPEACH.

Christ speakes to his Spouse.

THOU art my spouse, most chast, most pure   1
  Whom all the world doth loue:
Thou art my deere, my peere, my ioy,
  Noe spott in thee my doue.

Those that doe looke and see thy face   2
  Do praise and plaud thee still,
And bless thee that hast God thy Lord,
  And didst yeald to his will.

And thus they say, rapt with thy state   3
    What's shee, so faire as morne ?
So pure as sūne, so bright as mone,
    Of what state is shee borne ?

Her face is faire through force of faith,   4
    She is most bright in heue :
Yea in her looks is feare and dread
    To cause her foes to rue.

The Spouse speakes to Christ.

And thus all gast[1] and rapt with sight
    Of thy sweet port[2] and state,
They stand in stond all pale and wan,
    For thee they can not mate.

Noe more then glympse of starr cā dashe   6
    The sūne in height of skye,
Or light on earth, the mone at full
    Can darke, or once come nigh.

Cheare vp thy selfe my loue I say,   7
    For though thou didst me miss,
I meaue not thee my loue to leaue,
    For all the world that is.

---

[1] Transition-form of 'aghast'. G.
[2] = carriage, or behaviour. See former note. G.

THE SEUENTH SPEACH.

Christ speakes to his Spouse.

I DID but go to see my vine 1
   Howe it did bud and sprout,
To see what fruits my plants did yeald
   And howe they were come out.

And nowe I see they bud and blooe, 2
   And yeald me fruit good store :
Ile care for them, and they for me,
   That they may haue the more.

The soules that came to me of late, 4
   I prune, I plash,[1] I purge,
That they may bring forth farre more fruite
   With this my rod, and scourge.

And nowe they are well growne my deere, 5
   I hast, I runne to thee ;
With speed at need I hast, I post,
   With wings of wind to see.

What thou dost want, or wouldst nowe haue 6
   Speake loue, I'le giue thee it.

---

[1] Qy = to water, and hence as in Shakespeare, ' a shallow *plash* ' (Taming of Shrew 1. i.) but THOMAS WRIGHT says 'To interweave branches of a tree: to cut and lay a hedge'. G.

Thou shalt not feare my loue to thee,
  In rest by thee I'le sitt.

Come then my loue to me full fast,   6
  Let all saincts ioy and sing:
To house of God I'le safe and sound
  My deere shall my loue bring.[1]

Nowe all ye saincts and soules on high   7
  Looke, see, fixe fast your eie,
On this my loue; marke well her grace,
  No fault in her I spie.

---

[1] The meaning is clear, though here and elsewhere, the grammatical structure be faulty. G.

A Canticle, or Song.

Of the seuenth, & eight chapters of the song of Solomon being Metaphrased into Monosylabls of great Brittains language, & is to be vsed by euery deuout soule in his priuat
conference with
his god
And is sett to the tune of
Giue thanks vnto the lord our god.

Psal. cvii.

To his much esteemed good frend, Mr. WILLIAM WALCOT, marchant, one of the most worthie cōpanie of Marchant Adventurers, residing at Hamborough.

Happiness for euer.

KIND frend, Forced fauours were euer sleighted and thankles. But voluntary respects had euer with the best and most noble minds, courteous acceptāce, howe small and meane soeuer the thing was. For a ma to giue his soule to his Creator when he sees he must dye, and his goods to the poore, when he sees he must part with them; and to forgoe our sinne, whē we can noe longer followe yt, are cold, yea vnkind obediences. But for a young man to remember his creator in the daies of his youth, aud in his best and strongest age to bequeath himself euery day to God in prayer and praise, is that reasonable and seasonable sacrifice where with the Most High is most pleased. To this purpose, and noe other, God knoweth, I haue tendered these voluntary Essaies to diuerse of my masters and table-brothers. Let me not seeme to be officious, while I desire to doe good, and expresse my loue. For as vnto the rest so vnto you, Beloued,[1] haue I sent this parcell Receaue yt, as I meane yt, both with hand and hart, and then I am assured, it will neuer repent you of your acceptation, nor me of my dedication. The great Lord keeper of heauen and earth keepe you in his feare all the daies of your life, and preserve you for his sauving mercies in Christ Jesus in the end of your life and for euer.

Yours in Christ to be required,

W. LOE.

---

[1] An unintelligible word follows here, viz 'Gā-naunt'. G.

THE FIRST SPEACH.
Christ speaketh.

HER feet are sweet, her gate a grace,   1
    All shod with Peace and Truth,
Of God's owne spell to runne the race
    Frō bane, and woe, and ruth.

Her loynes are girt fast with the same,   2
    The price of it is rare,
The skill is framd with hand of might,
    All full of cost and care.

Her wombe like a round cup that wants   3
    Noe wine to cheere her plants;
As heaps of wheate set all with flowers,
    Pure graynes to helpe our wits.

Her breast the two sweet leagues of grace   4
    Are as to twins of birth,
Whose milke doth feede the babs of God
    Which dwell here on the earth.

Those that doe rule, and guide her folke   5
    Like necke doth beare vp head:

So those doe stay as tower of strength
   Till they at full are fed.

Her eies are like two fonts most cleare
   In which we may well see   6
Our selues in face, in fact, in faith,
   And drawe thence life and glee.

Her nose from whence we sent¹ the good   7
   Is as some tower of state,
For she can iudg and find it out
   From tyme to tyme past date.

THE SECOND SPEACH.

Christ speakes still.

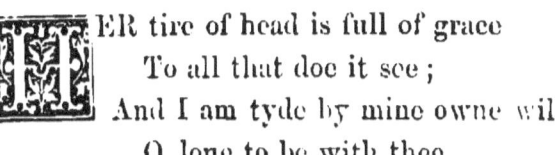ER tire of head is full of grace   1
   To all that doe it see ;
And I am tyde by mine owne will
   O lone to be with thee.

O loue howe full in all thy parts
   Dwells loue and life by me :
Howe sweet and faire art thou
   When I doe looke on thee.

Thy growth is like a palme tree tall,
   For prest, thou dost rise more :

---

1 Scent. G.

Thy teats are full of milke and mirth,
  And yeald thy babes great store.

I said I will goe to my tree   4
  And ioyne me to my palme,
And make it yeald all salues for sores
  To cure all wounds, as balme.

Christ speach still.

And I will cause her for to yeald   5
  Good workes of faith and life;
And with her power to driue frō her
  The sinnes that are so rife.

The soules that thirsts shall haue their fill,   6
  Her words shall spring as wine:
By mouthes of those that teach my lore,
  And preach those lawes of mine.

Yea they shall cause the lipps of him
  That sleeps and snorts in sinne   7
To speake, and praise the God of life
  That rouzd him from that din.

THE THIRD SPEACH.

The Church speakes.

SUCH as I am, I am not mine, 1
    But his that loud me deere.
In none but him will I be glad,
    None but him will I feare.

For he once gaue him selfe for me, 2
    And made of me his choyce.
Him will I heare, he is my deere,
    It's life to heare his voice.

O come my loue, letts lodg all night 3
    In fields; in townes, letts goe,
And see how all our flockes doe feede
    Letts runne as swift as roe.

Vp to the vines letts hast in morne, 4
    And vewe howe they doe bud,
And see the signes of fruits and grace,
    And looke if they be good.

For hence we shall knowe full our tyme 5
    When we shall ioyne in one,
In all the blisse that I haue made
    To quitt thee of thy mone.

See loue thy plants both in them selues 6
    Doe bud and bloome most fresh,

And yeald a sent to mōe them by
   That are but young, and neshe.¹

All plants that growe in vs I keepe,   7
   Both old and young I loue;
And all for thee O Christ my God
   Thy grace and lookes to moue.

THE FOURTH SPEACH.

The old Jewish Church speaketh.

 THAT I might my Christ once see   1
   Clad in this flesh of mine,
And find him here on earth to dwell
   Made once, once of my liue.

Thē would I kisse and cull my deere   2
   The world could not me touch;
But if it did I would not passe,
   Nor think of it too much.

Then would I bring thee to the light
   Though nowe pent vp in darke,
And then thou shouldst me teach to know
   My Christ, my God, by marke.

---

¹ = tender: query, transition-form of nice?'   G.

Then would I feast thee with the best 4
   With cupps of loue and grace,
Thē would the soules in Chiist be glad
   To vewe our rest and place.

The old Jewish Church speaketh.

His left hand then should stay my head, 5
   His right hand stay my hart,
And thē I would not feare the world
   Nor hell nor death, his dart.

His heat would giue me life halfe dead,
   And raise me vp cleane gone;
His light would make me shine like pearle:
   O like him there is none.

I charge ye O ye saincts that loue 7
   Dare not to greeue my deere,
Nor once to stirre him vp in ire,
   But lerne his wrath to feare.

THE FIFT SPEACH.

Christ speaketh.

WHO is this that from deuns of sinne
   From lusts and life most leaud,
Doth band her selfe gainst all the ill,
   And shewes her wrath and feud.

I'st not my church? O it is shee 2
   Whom I haue loud of old!
And did her take from powers o: hell
   When she was bought and sold.

And her frō ire of sinne and shame 3
   Where shee had falne from me,
I raisd to life from depth of hell
   I quitt, I sett her free.

For there by faith she leand on me, 4
   And I to her gaue way.
Then shee to me did ope her hart,
   And thus to me did say.

The Jewisch [sic] *Church speaketh.*

O sett me as a signe, a seale 5
   On hart, on arme, on all,
O hold me deere, my loue, my Christ
   For I to thee doe call.

Let naught me moue from my sweet loue
   Lest greefe me gore, and woe,
For the least shade when thou art gone
   Doth shew to me my foe.

The zeale where with I loue my deere 7
   Is like the graue most fell,

And burnes me vp like coles of fire,
  To saue my soule from hell.

THE SIXT SPEACH.

The Jewish Church speaketh.

YEA more then fire or flame it is   1
  Noe source can quench this loue,
Noe paines, noe gaines, or loss, or crosse
  From him my hart can moue.

Noe wealth, noe peelfe, noe feare, no force   2
  All this I scorne should me
Once moue, to thinke, or ioy in ought
  But in his grace and glee.

We haue a plant, deere loue thou knowst   3
  The church that thou hast chose,
From out the iles so farre frō hēce:
  O we would not her lose.

She is but smale of growth as yet,   4
  For want of thy good grace;
But if thou cast a looke on her,
  And let her see thy face.

Howe fresh, howe faire will she come forth, 5
  And growe, and beare to thee

Her buds, her bloomes, her fruites of faith
All good, and faire to see.

Christ speaketh.

If she be firme and fast to me,   6
  As wall, as tower of strength
I'le make her pure and sure in league
  By word and deed at length.

And if she will giue way to me,   7
  And to my words giue care,
I'le make her safe in league of peace,
  And she shall be my deere.

THE SEUENTH SPEACH.

The Jewish Church speaketh.

THE faith and loue that thou dost seeke   1
  In her, thou findst in me,
My plea of faith found grace and peace,
  And I was ioynd to thee.

The want of words to feed thy sainets   2
  Which thou in her dost craue
Is not in me to doe thy will,
  Howe then should she it haue.

Grãt thee to her thy grace in good,   3
    And shee will to thee bend ;
She will thee serue in word and deede
    If thou thy grace her send.

Christ speaketh.

My spouse is as a vine to me,   4
    She flowers and fruits doth yeald,
She is the corne that brings me thrift
    And growes faire in my feild.

The Jewish church speaketh

My vine shall aye be in my sight,   5
    Yea till the world haue end
I will it dress, and keepe my selfe,
    And grace and peace it lend.

Sith thus I care for thee my deere   6
    Shew thou thy loue in praise,
And teach my name, my fame to all,
    So long as last thy daies.

The Spouse speaketh.

If thou my deere wouldst haue me doe   7
    As thou hast bid to me,

Then grāt me grace to act the same
And thou it sone shalt see.[1]

---

[1] Following this are two blank leaves, as before; and on this page (164) the pagination ends. G.

A METAPHRASE.

Of the first, and second chapters of Jeremies Lamentations for the sacking and burning of Jerusalem, and the temple, by Nebuchadnezer king of Babell, and by Nebuzaradan the captaine of his gard, put into monsyllables of great Brittains language.

And is set to the tune of
I lift mine hart to thee.

Psal. XXV.

To his much esteemed good frend, Mr. EDWARD MEEDE, one of the assistants of the most worthy companie of Merchants-Aduenturers, residing at Hamborough.

Grace in this world, and ioy in the other.

ALL happines in the Lord Iesus, I present vnto you a part of Ieremie's Lamentations metaphrased. You may see herein my true heart vnto you all. In the midst of lamenttable discōtents I tuned my soule, tongue and pen, to the laud of God: and the rather in these Lamentations, for that they sorted some what to my retired meditations. One tyme or other all men are not as they would be. It is the condition of God's children. Happie is that man that can vse God's scourge to his amendment. The great Moderator of all things, knowes his children fittest to be made palmes, to be spread with burthens and waights, and not to be oliues. That so we might more think of our victorie, then of our rest. It is enoughe for vs that we shall once triumph in heauen and rest for all. To this holy rest and eternall tranquillity, God giude vs all, into whose blessed keeping I recommend you in Christ sauing mercies, and rest,

Yours much deuoted,

W LOE.

THE FIRST DEPTH.

Frō dumps and doomes of woe
   From depth of wrath and ire,
We call, we crie, we roare O Lord,   Aleph.
   With zeale as hot as fire.

The State where once thy name
   Was great in light of grace,
Is led a slaue by force of warre :   Beth.
   A curse is in the place.

Our streeats that flockt with folke
   Most rich, in cloths most gay,
Are nowe made void, and laid full wast Gimel.
   By night, and eke by day.

We that did rule and raigne,
   And brusd the world with might,
Doe nowe pay taxe, and tole, and disme[1]
   By force of armes, in spight.

---

[1] Tithe or tenth. Once used by Shakespeare, " many thousand *dismes*" (Troilus and Cress., ii, 2.) G.

We weepe full sore all night,
 By day our teares doe fall :   He.
Our eies are sore, our cheekes are wett,
 Yet on the Lord we call.

They that did loue vs once,
 And were our frends in shewe,
Are turnd to gall, and doe vs kill   Van.
 As feree as doth our foe.

THE SECOND DEPTH.

OUR prince is made a slaue
 To sitt with folke most base ;
We find noe rest but woe and moane,   Zain
 And shame doth fill our face.

Our sinne, our sinne hath greeud
 The Lord of hosts full sore.
Our shame, our shame for that doth come,   Heth.
 On vs nowe more and more.

Our things of worth the foe
 Hath seizd all to his hand,
They staine the church of thy great
   name   Teth
 We cā them not with stand.

The facts that we haue done
  Are all filths in his sight,
He pluckes vs downe, and none doth build,   Jod.
  Not one will doe vs right.

We sighe for bread in want
  We giue our wealth for yt :
O helpe sweete Lord for we are vile,   Caph.
  O drawe vs from this pitt.

O let all those that passe
  Looke on my woe, and see
If ere they sawe the like of this   Lamed.
  That nowe is done to me.

THE THIRD DEPTH.

IN all my bones is fire,
  A net my feete hath caught :
God turnes his face, and makes me
      faynt,   Mem.
  His wrath it hath me taught.

His hand is on my necke,
  His yoke hath bound me sore,
He beares his ha̅d so hard on me   Nun.
  That I can rise noe more.

My men of force are gone,
 My young men crusht with might,
My maids and babes are trod to dust Samech.
 And all this in my sight.

For these things, weeps myne eies,
 My soule is farre from glee :
The foe doth force me to this woe,   Ain.
 And none doth care for me.

We stretch our hands for helpe,
 And none doth take a care,
We are as is the filth of all,   Pe.
 They looke not howe we fare.

Yet thou art iust O Lord,
 For we haue gone from thee :
Thou wilt vs helpe for this at last :   Zade.
 O shewe thy face to me.

THE FOURTH DEPT. [sic]

MY preests gaue vp the ghost
 While they did seeke for meate, Koph.
The old men eke gave vp their breath :
 O Lord our woe is great.

I am in greefe O Lord,
  Mine hart is fild with woe:
The sword doth kill, and Death doth
    rage,   Resch
  For that thou art my foe.

When I doe sigh and grone
  Noe eie doth care for me:
My foes doe ioy, and glad themselues,   Shin.
  My woe and moane to see.

O let my sighes O Lord,
  Loud crie make in thine eares:
I haue done ill, cleāse me of that   Thau.
  And rid mine eies frō teares.

O Lord why with a cloud,
  So black of wrath and ire,   Aleph.
Hast thou vs clad, and càst vs downe:
  Why are we burnt with fire?

The Lord doth raze our race,
  Our stocke, our flocke, our all;
Downe to the ground, he dings[1] vs fast: Beth.
  Our prince, our peeres doe fall.

---

[1] See a former foot-note. G.

THE FIFT DEPTH.

THE strength of all our house   Gimel.
    Is spent, yea all is gone:
The Lord's ferce wrath hath cut vs of,
    To helpe vs there is none.

He bends his bowe at vs   Daleth.
    He shootes vs through full sore:
He kills the choice of all our flocke:
    O Lord what wilt thou more?

Our forts of fence and strength,
    Our fields so fresh, so full,   He.
Are all laid wast; our goods, our babes,
    Our foes from vs doe pull.

The king and preest at once   Van.
    The Church and State doe waile,
The daies of feasts are turnd to fasts,
    The Lord he doth vs quaile.

The Lord hath cast downe all,   Zain.
    They roare, and make a noice,
With in thy house O God our king,
    Where once was hard our voice.

Our wall, our wealth, our state,   Heth.
    Our God will lay full low.

His hand is bent to stricke vs all:
Thy will O Lord is so.

THE SIXT DEPTH.

THE lawe, and all is gone,   Teth.
  Noe preest, noe peere of light:
The Lord hath rid vs of them all,
  Not one doth come in sight.

The graue men of our State   Iod.
  The sage, and such as giude,
Doe sitt on groūd in dust and clay,
  With sacke they cloth their side.

Mine eies to see this, faile.   Caph.
  With teares they drope and melt:
The babes doe sowne[1] in midst of street,
  Such woe, and want they felt.

They crie for bread, for drinke   Lamed.
  To all that stand them nighe:
And in their lapps that gaue thē sucke
  They faint, and faile, and die.

What woe is like to ours?   Mem.
  Our breach as seas doe roare:

---

[1] = swoon   G

There's none can helpe or heale our wound
   O Lord our greefe is sore.

They that should see and say,   Nun.
   And tell vs of our sinne,
Haue taught vs things both vile and vaine,
   Noe good we find there in.

All such as pass vs by   Samech.
   Do scoffe at vs and mocke:
Is this the place say they of strength?
   Is this the whole Earth's rocke.

THE SEVENTH DEPTH.

OUR foes doe hisse and gnash   Ain.
   Their teeth, and thus doe saye:
This is the day we haue sought for
   To bring thee downe for aye.

But Lord this is thine acte   Pe.
   To throwe vs downe each one:
In days of old it was thy will
   To bruise vs bone by bone.

Our teares doe shower on vs   Zade.
   To thee our harts doe cry,
By day and night we take noe rest
   Our soules doe faint and dye.

We crye out in the night   Koph.
    Like babes we hold vp hands:
We faint for want of bread, O Lord
    O rid vs of these bands!

O see sweet Lord the babes   Resh.
    That are but a span long,
We cate for foode; our preests are slayne
    And cast out as the donge.

The young and old on ground   Shin.
    Are cast, and faint, and die:
Our maids so fresh, so faire in hewe
    Are kild, and cast them by.

Naught else but feares O Lord   Thau.
    Doe wake vs day and night:
It is the day of thy ferce wrath
    Of foes, of warre, of spight.

A Metaphrase.

OF THE THIRD Chapter of Jeremies Lamentations for the sacking and burning of Jerusalem, and the temple, by Nebuchadnezer king of Babell, and by Nebuzaradan the captaine of his gard, put into monosyllables of great Brittains language.

And is set to the tune of I lift mine hart to thee.

Psal. XXV.

To his much esteemed good frend, Mr. JOHN GREENWELL, on[e] of the Assistants of the most worthy companie of marchants-Aduenturers residing at Hamb:

All ioy, and happines in Christ.

WELBELOUED in the Lord, we are all strangers here in the Earth; our home is aboue in heauen. It was a great greefe to God's Israel to tune the songs of Sion in a strange country. Howe then is it with vs. that we like so well of the things here, and thinke not of the blessings aboue. Hierusalem was once the mistresse of the world, the metropolis of the earth, and yet when the world's darling forgatt God she was layd in the dust. That is the cause of the prophett's lamentation. Indeed who would not shower downe teares to see the holy place defiled, and Jerusalē made an heape of stones? But wee see noe place be it neuer so glorious in our eies, noe persons be they neuer so gratious in the sight of men, that can escape God's hand whē he will scourge. The Turkes haue encroched into

Christendome, and made that citty of Constantitinople which was once the glory of the East, a veary cage of vncleane Mahumetans. What Christian's hart doth not bleed to see yt? to heare of yt? We haue cause to lament this. The prophet had reason to condole that. O that our harts were touched with remorse for the poore distressed Christians that liue tributaries to the misbeleeuing Turke. Consider in these hymnes the condition of God's people so subjecte to moane and misery. God directe all our harts toward him in wealth, in woe, in all. And so I cōmending you to God with the rest, in the sauing mercies of Jesus Christ, am,

    Yours because of Christ.
        W. LOE.

THE FIRST DEPTH.

1. I AM the man O Lord
   Haue felt thy wrath, thy rod:
   O send me helpe in this my woe
   My Lord, my Christ, my God.

2. Thy stormes and clouds of ire
   Doe beate me day and night:
   Thou shewst me woe, and wast, and warre
   And hid'st from me the light.

3. All the day long O Lord
   Thine hand is turnd gainst me:
   Noe helpe, noe hope, noe ioy, noe mirth
   That I poore wretch can see.

4. My flesh and skin are vile,
   And parcht as in a drought;
   My bones, my hart are broke in twayne,
   This Lord thy wrath hath wrought.

5. O Lord thou mak'st a fort,
   With me to warre and fight
   With gall and greefe thou dost me fill
   And none will doe me right.

As they that long are dead,   6
And cleane cast out of mind,
So am I sett in night of death
With woe and greefe all pind.[1]

THE SECOND DEPTH.

N hedge is pight[2] me round   1
   To close me in this woe :
I can not stirre, thy chaines me bind :
   O Lord what shall I doe ?

And when I cry and roare,   2
   In all my greefe and gall
He shutts me out, and will not heare
   Ne cares he for my call.

He ramzes[3] me in so fast,   3
   With stones, and clay full thicke,
My pathes he crokes, and giues noe ease,
   My soule is faint and sicke.

As beares doe teare their pray,   4
   And waite more bloud to spill,

---

[1] Misnumbered 3, 5, onward, dropping 4, and so making seven stanzas (apparently) : corrected. G.

[2] Pitched, placed. G.

[3] Query—rammes = rams? G.

So hath my foes me rent and torne
   As if it were thy will.

I peece by peece, am hald,   5
   And puld by hand to raggs :
I by my selfe do sitt and weepe,
   While my foe sitts and braggs.

Thy bowe O Lord is bent,   6
   To shoote at my pale face :
I am a marke for shafts to hitt,
   O yett shewe me some grace !

THE THIRD DEPTH.

FOR see the shafts doe sticke,   1
   In all my raynes through out :
I am the butt, and none but I
   At which shootes all the rout.

My foes make me their iest   2
   And song by night and day ;
Where is thy God, thy Lord, thy helpe
   Thus they to me doe say.

Mine hart is fraught with gall,   3
   My bloud is drunke vp still :
With shame and greefe I waile and wast,
   Make hast me Lord to kill.

My strength is dasht, my teeth 4
Are broke with in my head:
Thou laist a¹ loade on me, poore soule,
I wish I were cleane dead.

My soule doth not once heare 5
Of peace, of grace, of light:
I can not call to mind my state
That once I had in sight.

O Lord my strength, my hope, 6
My helpe I looke from thee,
But all is gone, and there is none
That cares, nor lookes to me.

THE FOURTH DEPTH.

CALL to mind sweet God, 1
 This moane, this woe of mine,
This gall, this greefe, this plaint, this
 cry,
 For I O Lord am thine.

My soule is faint, and failes, 2
 When I to mind doe call:
My greefe hath made me cry and roare
 To see my woe and fall.

---

¹ Misprinted 'on'. G.

Yet haue I hope in thee   3
  That thou wilt helpe at last,
And wilt not quite my soule for aye
  From thy sweet sight out cast.

It is thy loue O Lord,   4
  That I am not quite sold,
And rid from earth, both braunch and roote,
  And closd vp in the mold.

Thou failst me not in morne,   5
  All night I feele thy stay;
Thy hand is great, and in thy truth
  Thou hearst what I doe say.

For thou O Lord art mine,   6
  My soule doth hope in thee:
Thou art my lot, my land, my rent:
  Once more, Lord sett m̀e free.

THE FIFT DEPTH.

THOU art good, O Lord   1
  To them that wayte and tend:
To soules that seeke and sue to thee
  Thou dost thy grace downe send.

It is right good O Lord 2
  To hope for helpe from thee :
For of thee Lord is all man's good :
  O shewe thy smile to me.

It is full good for man 3
  In youth to beare thy rod ;
For he shall learne there by to knowe
  The Lord to be his God.

Then sitts he pale and wan, 4
  And mute without a pecare :
He will take heed all tymes that he
  Doe scarne the Lord in feare.

And if he see there's hope 5
  His mouth from dust will cry ;
And to the Lord make plaint, and moane
  To day that he doth dye.

He giues his cheeke to such 6
  As smite him, and doe taunt :
He will not giue his eare to those
  That vaine and vile things chaunt.

THE SIXT DEPTH.

    THE Lord doth not for aye   1
      Cast of his choice of men,
    But though they greeue, yet in his tyme
      He brings them from that den.

For by his will the Lord   2
  Greeues not his flocke at all :
Nor doth he crush the sonnes of mē
  When they on him doe call.

He rights men in their ill :   3
  The face of the Most High
Is sett to helpe the flocke of Christ,
  Yea he will drawe them nigh.

Out of God's owne sweet mouth   4
  Comes forth not good, and ill :
When we are plagued it is our sinne
  That doth our deare soules kill.

Let vs then search our waies,   5
  And turne to our good God :
So shall he quite put farre from vs
  His scourge, his plague, his rod.

Lift vp both hand and hart   6
  To him that dwells on highe,

And shewe our sinns, our shame to him
Least that for him we dye.

THE SEUENTH DEPTH.

THOU hast vs slayne O Lord 1
   And hid'st vs with a cloud,
So that our sute comes not to thee,
   Though we doe cry full loud.

We are as drosse and doung, 2
   Our foes doe on vs rage :
A feare and snare is come on vs,
   And that from age to age.

Mine eies cease not to weepe 3
   But day by daye we moane :
Till thou O Lord dost looke from high,
   And ease vs of our grone.

My eies and hart doe ake, 4
   The one with teares doth runne,
My hart it sobbs, and sighes full sore
   For that which I haue done.

Men chase me like a bird, 5
   They haue cut of my life
They cast great stones to keepe me downe
   They kill me in their strife.

    Yet from these depths O Lord
        I haue cald on thy name: 6
    Thou to my voice wilt giue an eare
        And ease me of the same.

THE EIGHTH MUSE.

THOU wont'st to say, Feare not,   1
    Thou wont'st my cause to plead:
And to the streames of love and life
    Thou wast wont me to lead.

O Lord my wronge thou seest   2
    Judge thou my cause with those
That gape, and hope to eate me vp:
    With rage they doe me close.

Thou Lord hast heard their cries   3
    Howe they doe rage, and roare:
Howe they doe spite and spitt at me,
    And raue still more and more.

They make their songs on me   4
    They iest, and gibe, and mocke:
When they sitt downe, or rise, or walke
    They flout, they feare thy flocke.

Giue them their lott O Lord,   5
    Looke on the worke they wrought:

Giue them thy curse with greefe of hart,
That haue my woe thus sought.

Cast them all cleane from thee 6
Let not the Earth them beare,
For that they doe not seeke to thee
But rage with out all feare.

A METAPHRASE.

Of the fourth, and fift Chapters of Ieremies Lamentations for the sacking, & burning of Ierusalem, and the temple, by Nebuchadnezer king of Babell, and by Nebuzaradan the captaine of his gard, put into monosyllabeles of great Brittains language.

*And is set to the tune of
I lift mine hart to thee.*

PSALM XXV.

THE FIRST DEPTH.

HOWE is our gold so dymme?
The fine gold howe is't lost?
The stones of the Lord's house are wast,
This is our case, our cost.

Our sonnes that were so strong   2
  Are trod as clay in streete,
And as the potts so are they broke,
  They crush them with their feete.

The formes of fish in sea,
  That are most strange to see,
Yea they to young ones yeald their breasts:
  With vs this may not bee.

The babe that suckes is drye,   4
  For bread the young ones cry,
But bread and breast they can haue none
  And so they faint and dye.

They that did feede most fine   5
  The crusts most course would haue;

To his much esteemed good frend Mr. IONS STAMPE, marchant, one of the cōpanie of the Marchants - Adventurers, residing at Hamborough.

Eternall blisse in Christ Jesus.

MINE unfained loue in Christ vnto you: Noe wise man would sell his thoughts for all the world. For as they are much pleasing to a man's selfe so are they beneficiall vnto others. I little thought whē I began to make an Essay into this businesse that it would haue enlarged it selfe into eleuen branches. What it is, and as it is; euen the all of it, I devote to all my table-brothers; wherein your selfe haue a part. I shall desire your acceptance with the rest. And euen so herein I commēd my loue to you, my lines to the world's censure, and the vse of thē to God's children; for whose sake I haue endeuored this. Thus with my prayers for your successfull prosperity in all things I leaue you to God's sauing grace. *Remay[n]ing*
      Your affectionate,
        W. LOE.

They that put on their robs of silke,
The pigs coote¹ seekes, and craue.

The woe that we doe here 6
Is farre more great then when
our God did rayne fell fire fr̄osk·y,
And burnt the sonnes of men.

THE SECOND DEPTH.

HEY that were pure as snowe, 1
And white as is the milke,
And lookt so red, so fresh, so faire,
And clad them selues with silke,

They are as blacke as cole, 2
By face they are not knowne;
Their skin is parcht, and cleaues to bones,
They waile, they weepe, they moane.

They whom the sword doth kill 3
We count in a good case;
For they that liue doe pine for want,
Both they and all their race.

The babes that sucke the breast 4
We seeth for meat in pott,

---

¹ = cot or stye. G.

Or else we pine for want of meate,
  Our limbs doe fade and rott.

The Lord is wrath with vs, 5
  On vs he shoures his ire,
And we are cleane put out of sight,
  He burnes vs vp with fire.

The kings of all the earth 6
  Doe stand in maze to see:
Our foes march in our streats with routs,
  And we poore soules to flee.

THE THIRD DEPTH.

BUT this is come to vs 1
  For that we shed the blond
Of such as were most neere to God,
  And shewd vs all the good.

The blond I say of them 2
  Doth cry gainst vs to God,
And nowe we feele his hand of ire,
  His scourge his whipe, his rod.

This blond of men so iust, 3
  Hath bine our bane, our woe,
And made vs turne our backes frō such
  As made them selues our foe.

For we car'd not for preeste, 4
  Nor those that did vs good,
But were both ferce and fell to them,
  We stroue to sheed their bloud.

For this our eies doe watch 5
  And waite, and still doe faile,
No helpe, no hand is stretcht to vs,
  And so we fainte and quaile.

The foe doth hunt our stepps 6
  As we goe in the streete:
They kill, they cry, they roare on vs,
  They tread vs with their feete.

THE FOURTH DEPTH.

HEY hunt vs in the feilds, 1
  On hills, in dales they kill;
We dare not once loke out of dore,
  Our streats with dead they fill.

The breath of all our liues 2
  Is caught fast in their snare,
And left he is in plight full ill,
  Both base, and poore, and bare.

Let these be glad that dwell 3
  Farre of[f] out of this place:

Take heede least you doe moue the Lord,
  Gainst you to turne his face.

For he hath plagued vs sore   4
  For all our sinnes and ill,
And yet we hope he will loke back
  And cease our folke to kill.

The V. Cap.

O Lord call thou to mind
  What is come on vs all:
Take heede to vs that in our woe
  To none but thee doe call.

Our lands, our rents, our all   6
  The foe from vs doe take.
The folke that are to vs most strange,
  A prey of vs doe make.

THE FIFT DEPTH.

OUR babes doe know noe sires,   1
  And they that gaue the breast
  Doe sitt, and sighe, and roare, and cry,
Ne can they like their rest.

Our drinke to vs is sold,   2
  Our wood we buy full deare;

And all this ill is come on vs,
  For thee we did not feare.

Our neckes are prest with yokes,   3
  On vs they lie full sore :
We moile, and toyle, and haue noe rest :
  O Lord what wilt thou more.

To those that be our foes,   4
  For bread we giue our hands :
They tire on vs, and make a prey,
  They breake in to our lands.

They that are dead, and gone,   5
  O Lord haue done the sinne,
And wee poore soules doe pay the price,
  These take vs in their gin.

Base slaues whom we did beate,   6
  Ore vs now rule and tire ;
And there is none that doth vs helpe,
  Our feete stickes in the mire.

THE SIXT DEPTH.

OUR bread we gett with dread,   1
  It costs vs halfe our life :
We waile in midst of woe, and waste
  All night, all day in strife.

Our skin, like to a moore 2
   Is blacke for want of meate :
Our parts are parcht to skin and bone :
   Thy wrath O Lord is great.

Our maids they make a prey 3
   To serue their minds and lusts :
Our wiues they wrong in all our sights,
   Yet Lord thy hand is iust.

By hand our prince they hang, 4
   The old men they doe scorne :
Our greefe doth last till it be night,
   And eke till it be morne.

They make our young ones grind 4
   And toyle like horse in mill :
Their backes they load with batts[1] of wood
   Till that they doe them kill.

The old men sitt noe more 5
   To iudg the cause in gate :
The young mē waile that wont to sing :
   Oh when will be our date.

---

[1] Loads. G.

Our ioy of hart is gone, 6
    Our daunce is turnd to moane:
Our minds doe muse of nought but woe,
    We sitt, and sighe, and grone.

THE SEAUENTH DEPTH.

THE crowne is gone from vs, 1
    And all the rule is fled;
What shall we doe O Lord our God,
    Our sinne hath struck vs dead.

For sinne our hart is faynt, 2
    For sinne our eies are dymme;
For sinne our foes doe warre on vs,
    And rend vs limbe by limbe.

Our hills and dales are waste, 3
    The foxe doe roome and range;
These things to see our harts doe bleed,
    To vs it is most strange.

Yet Lord thou art for aye, 4
    Thy throne is sett full sure:
Thou can'st vs helpe, when hope is gone,
    O Lord nowe doe vs cure.

Why then dost hide thy face, 5
    And wilt not on vs looke?

Thou wilt at last thy grace vs giue,
　That is wrote in thy booke.

Turne to vs Lord we praye,　　　　　　6
　And then we shall see grace:
O giue to vs the daies of old,
　Thy name sett in this place.

What shall thy wrath like fire　　　　　7
　Still last, and burne, and kill:
O cease sweet Lord we doe thee pray
　So shalt thou find noe ill.

Seauen Dumpes

ON THE SEAUEN WORDS
that Christ spake on the crosse
which shewe the seauen depthes of the
   lawes curse, which our lord did
      feele for our sinnes.

>   *And is set to the tune of*
>   *I lift mine hart to thee.*
>   PSALM XXV.

To his much esteemed good frend Mr. GEORGE FRANKLYN, on[e] of the Assistants of the most worthy companie of marchants-Adventurers residing at Hamb :

Grace here, Glory hereafter, in Christ.

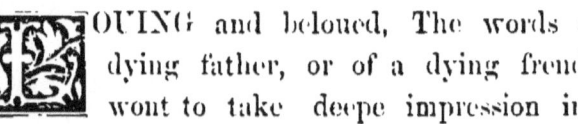OVING and beloued, The words of a dying father, or of a dying frend are wont to take deepe impression in the minds and memories of good natures. Whose words shall pearce, if the words of our Christ, our dying Christ, and that for vs, and his last also : Whose I say if not his ? To you I send the last words of Christ, in the last place, yet you are not the least in my loue. The first in intention is last in execution. And nothing is conveayed to the intellectuall powers that is not first in the sensible parts. It was God's purpose of our Christ, euen in the creatiõ, that he should be thus vpon the crosse. See then your Christ at his last. Tune your dolefull dumps to a sad soule, and ioy in sobbs. For he prayes, cries, yells, promiseth, perfecteth all, that we may be all in all with God.

What can be more? Christ passion is the modell of our profession, yea the medall of our perfection. For God's strength is perfected in our weakenes.

We may sowe in teares, we shall reape in ioy. Let my Spring be wett so that I may haue a plentifull Autume I care not. *Vir dolorum* can best tune his voice to dolours. If God will haue it so, His will be done. He did so with his owne. We cannot imagine our condition free. God giude vs through all by his sauing grace, to which I shall euer recommend you, and rest,

Your more then much affectionate,

W. Loe.

THE VEWE.

 GOD my soule lift vp,   1
   And stretch mine hart in twaine,
That it may feele, and faile, and die,
   For life is in this paine.

My poore heart is so full   2
   And fraught with thought of thee,
That it's nighe rent to see thy loue
   So much, so maine for me.

O take thy crosse and nailes,   2
   And straine my hart at length,
That thy deere loue may not be pent,
   But shewe my soule my strength.

And nowe my thoughts are free   3
   Thy loue to vewe in sight,
My hart doth pant, for that noe more
   It feeles here of thy might.

O fill my hart once more,
   And stretch and straine it still,

That I may lothe and loue no more
   My sinne that brought this ill.

But I want space in hart, 6
   And grace in all my life,
To end my smart in sight of this,
   And sinnes that are so rife.

But since my hart O God 7
   Holds not a sight of thee,
O doe thou Lord hold fast my hart
   And shewe thy loue to me.

THE FIRST DUMPE: ON THE FIRST WORD.

Father forgiue them for they knowe not what they doe.—
LUCK. 23. VERSE 34.

WHAT voice is this so shrill 1
   That soūds thus in mine eare?
O put from them their sinns O God
   That knowes not what's thy feare.

Is't not thy voice O Christ, 2
   On crosse when thou didst hang?
And eke for those that did thee kill,
   Is't not thy voice that sang?

A tune to God on highe 3
  With which his care was pleasd,
To see thy deere loue stretch so farre,
  And made the world so eas'd.

They knewe not what they did: 4
  Was ere such a thing seene?
To pray for those that made a prey
  In woes so sharp so keene.

O soule full oft thou hast 5
  Not knowen what thou hast done:
Noe way for helpe to cure that greefe
  But in thy Christ, God's sonne.

O pray my soule for them 6
  That hate thee to the graue,
And let not wrath lodg with thee once,
  It's Christ that must thee saue.

When foes doe curse, blesse them 7
  For Christ hath taught thee so;
Who prayd for such as did him kill
  And brought to curse and woe.

THE NEXT DUMPE : ON THE NEXT WORD.

Verily I say vnto thee, This day shalt thou be with me in paradice.—Luck 23. v. 43.

SOULE looke vp to this,   1
   And harke what voice thou hear'st;
Thy Christ in midst of gripes of death
   Doth heare, what is't thou fearst?

Then sure he will thee heare,   2
   And giue eare to thy crye,
Nowe that he sitts on throne in state
   And is thy God so nighe.

A theefe doth cry and call,   3
   Christ heares him by and by :
O soule thy Christ will heare thee sure
   If thou dost call and cry.

O learne it is but one   4
   To whom Christ grants an eare,
That sued to him in death at last,
   And sought him in his feare.

Yet it is one my soule   5
   Least thou shouldst faynt and dye,
And that thy Christ would not thee heare
   In death when thou shalt cry.

And yet it is but one,   6
  Least soule thou shouldst be proud,
And thinke that God would heare thee still
  When that thy cry is loud.

O learne sweet soule by this   7
  To sue to God in life,
And driue not of[f] till death doe come
  To die in iarre and strife.

THE THIRD DUMPE: ON THE THIRD WORD.

Behold thy mother, Behold thy sonne.
JOHN 19. v. 26, 27.

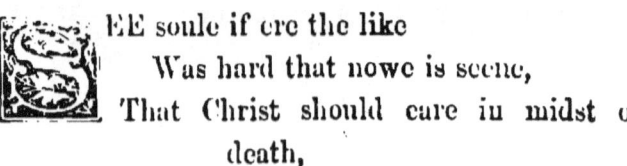EE soule if ere the like   1
  Was hard that nowe is seene,
That Christ should care in midst of death,
  And greefes that were so keene

For those that could not helpe,   2
  But sawe him in that plight,
Burst soule and die, to see his loue
  To her that bare his might.

And eke to him whose loue   3
  Was fixt sure in his breast:

That Christ should care in midst of greefe
That he should liue in rest.

She that whose seede did bruse, 4
    The head of hell and death,
Hath hart all prest with woe and greefe
    To see Christ lose his breath.

O child see that thou loue, 5
    And loke, and long for good,
To those that haue thee borne and bred,
    And are thee nighe in bloud.

Shall not our Christ loue those 6
    Thinke you that searue him still,
And haue a care of all such folke
    That seeke to doe his will.

My soule they are all deare 7
    He cares for all their seede,
Ne shall there one that serues our God
    Be void of his full meede.

THE FOURTH DUMPE: ON THE FOURTH WORD.

My God, my god, why hast thou forsaken me?
MAT. 27. vers. 46.

 NOWE my soule giue care   1
   To this great cry and yell,
That shakes the heauens and moues the earth
   And teares the powers of hell.

My God, my God cries Christ   2
   Why putts thou me thee fro,
And why dost hide thy face frō me
   As if I were thy foe.

O soule he cries for thee,   3
   That thou maist haue God's light,
And nere be cast in pit full lowe,
   And hid out of his sight.

This cry did darke the sunne   4
   In full smyle of his beames:
O soule doth not it dymme thy sight,
   And cause of teares full streames?

My soule great is our sinnes   5
   That causd these groanes and cries:

My eares that heare, are dull and deafe,
   My hart it faynts, and dies.

What paine didst thou O Christ   6
   For me base wretch then beare,
That thou didst yell, and cry, and roare
   In such great greefe and feare.

Wast not that I might nere   7
   Feele God goe from my hart?
Wast not O Christ that I might not
   Of hell once feele the smart.

THE FIFT DUMPE: ON THE FIFT WORD.

I thirst.—John 19, v, 28.

WHAT thirst was this O Christ   1
   That thou di'st feele so fell?
   That made thee call for drinke in drought,
   That causd thee thus to yell?

Wast not for my poore soule   2
   Thou didst cry in thy thirst?
That I might tast these streames of ioy
   That man had at the first.

And nere to thirst for aye, 3
    But haue the streames full glad,
That ioy the hart, and soule, and all,
    And blesse the mind that's sad.

Thou art the rocke O Christ 4
    From whence the source doth flowe
That makes vs feele no thirst at all
    But vp wards for to growe.

Come to this source my soule, 5
    And drench thy deepe sad mind,
Thou cãst not chuse but here thou must,
    A well of blisse sure find.

For Christ didst thirst for thee 6
    That thou mights[t] drinke I say,
The streames that flowe from throne of God
    Where Christ doth dwell for aye.

All soules doe thirst for this 7
    All sainets for this doe crye,
And bray as harts doe for the flouds,
    And so to faynt and dye.

THE SIXT DUMPE.

It is finished.—JOHAN. 19. VERS. 30.

NOWE all is done my soule   1
    That can be done for thee,
The houres of death and powers of hell
    Are all put farre from me.

Christ nowe hath paid the debt,   2
    The bond in two is rent,
The lawe, the curse, the woe, the crosse
    Is laid on him that's sent.

Loe Christ hath tane for thee   3
    Thy sinne, thy shame, thy crosse,
And rid thee from the bags of hell
    That would haue wrought thy losse.

Nowe is the world all iudged: 4
    All powers of death and hell
Haue done their worst, and nowe in woe
    Doe cry, and roare, and yell.

It's done, it's done, saith Christ!   5
    Ye[a] all is past and cleare,
That thou my soule maist liue in blisse
    And be to God most deare.

Is this the way O Christ,   6
  That we tast woe with thee,
That so we may once rule and raigne,
  And thy sweete face still see.

O lett thy will O Lord,   7
  Be done of vs in fine,
And by vs let thy will be done
  That still we may be thine.

THE SEVENTH DUMPE: ON THE SEVENTH WORD.

Father into thy hands doe I commend my spirit.
LUCK. 23. VERS. 46.

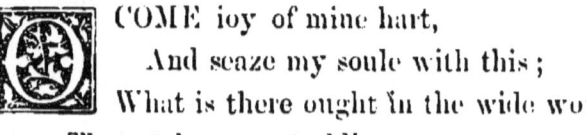COME ioy of mine hart,   1
  And seaze my soule with this;
What is there ought in the wide world
  That cā be more to blisse

Then for my soule to heare
  My Christ his soule to giue,
Into the hands of God my Lord
  There still for aye to liue?

Nowe soule, thou seest thy blisse,   2
  And where thou maist be sure,

To haue thy rest, thy ioy, thy stay
   Thy loue, thy life, thy cure.

O blest are they that dye,   4
   They rest from all their care;
When once the Lord doth sett them free,
   What Death or Hell can dare?

In his, O soule, thy Christ   5
   For thine made suite to God
Thou need'st not feare the day of death
   Nor graue, nor hell, his rod.

For thou art safe in him   6
   That keepes thy life in store,
And it is hid in Christ, thy Lord,
   What can'st thou wishe nowe more?

O soule die in these words,   7
   Giue vp thy selfe in fine
To God in Christ, and feare no ill
   For he saies 'Thou art mine'.

TO HIM THAT MADE THESE HYMNS.

WHEN with my thoughts I vewe thy saynct like Muse
    How on[e] while drencht in sobs, and sighs for sinne;
And yet more low, the paths of death doth vse;
There seisd with greef, yet prayes: then sours¹ euen in
Heauen's gate it self: and there true loue doth find,
And then it's Christ doth see, and vew: his payne,
His cross: his speare-pearst side, his greef of mind
Thence dumpt twixt ioy and greef: as on[e] half slayne
I muse, euen at thy muse, how well, how fit it lymms
It's greef, sobs, sighs and tears, in tunes, in songs, and hymns.

                          J. P.

---

1 = soars. G.

TO HIM THAT MADE THESE HYMNS.

THER'S but one God, that this world one hath made
One Christ, one Truth, one faith, one hope, one loue;
To serve this one, in hymns of ones, dost shade
Thy zeale, to teach vs that in one we moue.
Loe, as thy hymns be ones, so is thy name but odd,
How fitt? both name and hymns doe ioyne to praise one God.
Thus ten and one, in one thou hast nowe framd,
That we in one should keep the lawe of ten;
Thus by seaven and seaven thou hast them so namd
For seaven tymes seaven, day by day, we break them.
Loe, your hymns, of one, ten and one, and seaven by seaven
Learns, God to laud, his lawe to keepe, the way to heauen.

G. F.[1]

---

[1] Query - Dr. Giles Fletcher, (*pater*)? G.

finis.

www.ingramcontent.com/pod-product-compliance
Lightning Source LLC
Chambersburg PA
CBHW032134160426
43197CB00008B/642